English Grammar Practice

English Grammar Practice

Raj N Bakshi

Orient BlackSwan

The author and publishers record their grateful thanks to the editor of this work:

Dr M Hariprasad
Centre for Linguistics and Contemporary English
School of Language Sciences
CIEFL, Hyderabad 500 007

English Grammar Practice

ORIENT BLACKSWAN PRIVATE LIMITED

Registered Office
3-6-752 Himayatnagar, Hyderabad 500 029, Telangana, India
email: centraloffice@orientblackswan.com

Other Offices
Bengaluru, Bhopal, Chennai, Guwahati, Hyderabad, Jaipur, Kolkata, Lucknow, Mumbai, New Delhi, Noida, Patna, Visakhapatnam

First published 2005
Reprinted 2007, 2009, 2016, 2017, 2018, 2019

ISBN: 978 81 250 2799 7

Typeset in Times 11pt by
OSDATA, Hyderabad 500 029

Printed in India at
The Print Park, Chennai 600 117

Published by
Orient BlackSwan Private Limited
3-6-752 Himayatnagar, Hyderabad 500 029, Telangana, India
e-mail: info@orientblackswan.com

CONTENTS

PREFACE

English Grammar Practice is a textbook for first year college students and senior secondary school students who need to study and use English for written and spoken discourse. It can also be used by students preparing for competitive examinations. This book concentrates on those areas of grammar which these students need to use but often find difficult. It covers a complete range of word classes, phrases, clauses, simple and complex sentences, tenses, prepositions, active and passive sentences, direct and indirect speech, etc. It will enable college and senior secondary school students to review and practise grammar structures.

The aim of the book is to focus on those areas of grammar that students find difficult, especially while using them in connected discourse. It consists of 54 units. Each unit deals with and concentrates on a particular point of grammar. An attempt has been made to explain a point of grammar as precisely as possible, helping students grasp the basic rules necessary for practising that given point. This will help students understand or review the rules of grammar presented in the unit. However, the main focus in each unit is on practising the given point of grammar. Therefore the explanation is followed by a large number of exercises to help students practise that point of grammar.

Exercises have been graded into three categories – elementary, intermediate and advanced. Elementary exercises help students practise a grammar structure without any difficulty. Intermediate exercises require the basic understanding of a grammar structure and advanced exercises require good competence in English. It is, therefore, required that the exercises in a unit are done in the order in which they have been presented.

This book can be used as a textbook in class by a teacher or it can be used as a self-study book. It is also possible for a teacher to use the explanation of a grammar structure in class, give some of the elementary exercises for self-study and use the other elementary, intermediate and advanced exercises for practice in class under supervision.

It is not necessary to work through the units in the order that they have been presented. It is up to the teacher to use the order that he/she feels will be most suitable for his/her students. It is possible to use the first 29 units from *Simple Sentences 1* to *Adverbs 3* in one semester or one academic year and units 30 to 54 from *Modal Verbs 1* to *Phrasal Verbs* in the second semester or second year.

It is hoped that this book will develop the confidence and competence of students to use connected discourse.

Raj N. Bakshi
Lucknow, 2004.

Unit 1

SIMPLE SENTENCES 1

The term 'grammar' is understood to mean rules which are used to combine words with each other to form sentences. Thus grammar means the study of word classes such as nouns, verbs, adjectives, adverbs, etc. Grammar also means the study of how these words are used to form phrases, how phrases are used to form clauses and how clauses are used to form simple and complex sentences.

The number of simple sentence patterns is small and limited. An English sentence must have a *subject* (often a noun or a noun phrase) and a *predicate*. The *predicate* could be a verb or a verb followed by an *object* or a *complement*.

Before we discuss *subject* and *predicate* further, read the following tables and make as many meaningful sentences as possible.

Table 1

Example: *The dog is barking.*

Subject	Verb
The dog The baby The tiger The bell Birds The girls Meera The boys The bomb Rakesh	rang. were playing. are singing. cries. is barking. was studying. is sleeping. roars. fly. exploded.

TABLE 2

Example: *Birds fly in the sky.*

Subject	Verb	Adverbial
Birds	writes	neatly.
The tiger	drives	on the table.
The baby	is parked	in the sky.
Varoon	were ringing	in our college.
She	fly	fast.
Your book	works	loudly.
The car	was lying	hard.
Her father	roars	in the garage.
The bells	work	on the floor.
They	slept	continuously.

TABLE 3

Example: *Mukesh was a doctor.*

Subject	Verb	Complement
Mukesh	is	a nurse.
Reema	are	a doctor.
Ashok and Rahul	has been	an officer.
I	was	a student.
Her father	am	teachers.

TABLE 4

Example: *Her shirt is red.*

Subject	Verb	Complement
Her shirt	was	talented.
Vanita	is	red.
Raj and Vijay	are	dangerous.
This dog		tall.
The book		interesting.

TABLE 5

Example: *She has been a doctor for five years.*

Subject	Verb	Complement	Adverbial
My mother	looks	good	for ten years.
Sunita	tastes	a general	next year.
Rina	has been	a nurse	with chocolate.
Milk	will become	bright	in a blue dress.
Her father		a doctor	for four years.

SUBJECT AND PREDICATE

A simple sentence in English consists of two parts: a *subject* and a *predicate.* Notice the division of these sentences into subject and predicate.

Subject	**Predicate**
(1) Birds	fly.
(2) Birds	fly in the sky.
(3) Madhuri	is a doctor.
(4) Rajesh	is tall.
(5) Madhu	is in the library.
(6) The dog	chased a rat.
(7) The old man	told us a story.
(8) The committee	elected him Mayor.
(9) He	dyed his shirt blue.

The above sentences illustrate that the subject of a sentence can be a noun *(Birds, Madhuri, Rajesh, Madhu)*, a noun phrase *(The dog, The old man, The Committee)* or a pronoun (*He*). The predicate is more complex than the subject. In sentence (1), the predicate is just the main verb *fly.* In sentence (2), however, the predicate consists of the main verb *fly* and the prepositional phrase *in the sky* which functions as the adverbial. Similarly, sentence (6) has the predicate *chased a rat* with *chased* as the main verb and *a rat* as the object. Thus we find that a predicate can have the verb or it can have the verb followed by several constituents.

EXERCISE 1 (ELEMENTARY)

Identify the subject and predicate in the following sentences.

1. Her youngest brother is a famous doctor.
2. The Finance Minister has given us tax concessions.
3. Meena runs very fast.
4. The food smells very good.
5. All the old employees are unhappy.
6. Her teachers consider her witty.
7. Rajneesh is sitting in the corner.
8. The Board's decision has made us happy.
9. The University has framed a new rule.
10. The old students have gone out for dinner.
11. Monica offered Ashok her car yesterday.
12. The tall boy standing in the corner is our captain.
13. He has grown tall.
14. That blue car is very old.
15. All the students sang well at the party.
16. Her father works in a bank.
17. My cousin looked splendid at the wedding.
18. All the girls watched TV in the evening.
19. Lions roar.
20. Krishna bought a briefcase yesterday.

THE CONSTITUENTS OF A SENTENCE

Subject

Every statement in English begins with a subject. The subject of a verb is usually a noun, a pronoun or a noun phrase. The subject noun, pronoun or noun phrase is tied to or is in agreement with the verb.

(10) The dogs are barking. The dog is barking.
(11) Lions roar. The lion roars.

Verb

The verb is the second constituent of a statement. There are three types of verbs:

- linking verb (see Pattern 2 S + LV + Cs for the explanation of the linking verb)

- intransitive verb (see Pattern 1 S + IntrV + (Adv) for the explanation of the intransitive verb)
- transitive verb (see Pattern 3 S + TrV + Od + (Adv) for the explanation of the transitive verb)

Complement

A complement usually follows a linking verb. The complement has the meaning of 'may be described as'. The complement tells us more about the subject. The subject and the complement refer to the same person or thing.

	S	LV	Cs
(12)	My father	is	a doctor.
(13)	My sister	is	tall.

See Pattern 2 for more examples of S + LV + Cs. However, sometimes an object can also have a complement. This means that a transitive verb requires a direct object and the direct object is followed by an object complement.

	S	LV	Od	Co
(14)	The players	chose	Varinder	captain.
(15)	Rakesh	considered	her	talented.

See Pattern 4 for more examples of S + TrV + Od + Co.

Object

Objects are of two types, *direct object* and *indirect object* and occur only after *transitive verbs.* If a transitive verb requires only one object, it has to be a direct object.

	S	TrV	Od	(Adv)
(16)	She	has read	this novel	recently.
(17)	Monica	cooked	dinner	in the evening.

An indirect object also comes immediately after the main verb but is usually followed by a direct object.

	S	TrV	Oi	Od
(18)	She	asked	him	a question.
(19)	Rita	told	us	a story.

For more examples and explanation of the object, see patterns 3, 4 and 4a.

Adverbial

An adverbial can be a one-word adverb, a noun phrase, a prepositional phrase or a clause.

(20) Ravinder lives *there.* (adverb)
(21) I read this novel *last week.* (noun phrase)
(22) Salma is sitting *in the library.* (prepositional phrase)
(23) I met him *while he was leaving the room.* (clause)

Basic Patterns

Pattern 1

Subject (S) + Intransitive Verb (Intrv) + Adverbial (Adv)

An intransitive verb denotes an action or event which does not refer to anything other than the subject. In other words, there is nobody or nothing to receive the action of the verb. However, one can add an *adverbial* after the intransitive verb.

	S	Intrv	Adv
(24)	Lata	fainted.	
(25)	She	laughed	loudly.

Exercise 2 (intermediate)

Arrange the following words under the order S + Intrv + (A). Remember to begin with a capital letter and end with a full stop.

1. in July / begins / our college
   Our college (S) begins (Intrv) in July. (A)
2. play / while their parents are away / they
3. Gita / with a pen / writes
4. till 10' clock yesterday / the children / slept
5. run / Vijay and Suresh / whenever they see a dog
6. arrived / late / the train
7. there / slept / I
8. soldiers / when they are on leave / rest

9. fast / she / ran
10. over the wall / jumped / I
11. cry / loudly / babies
12. studied / in the room / the boy
13. on the ice / Asha / slipped
14. on the mat / sleeps / Salma
15. continuously / the bombs / exploded

Pattern 2

Subject (S) + Linking Verb (LV) + Subject Complement (Cs) + Adverbial (Adv)

Unlike an intransitive verb, a linking verb requires a complement to complete the meaning of the sentence. Usually the complement after the linking verb qualifies the subject of the sentence. A complement that qualifies the subject is known as subject complement.

	S	LV	CS
(26)	They	were	happy.
(27)	That dog	is	dangerous.
(28)	Her father	has been	an officer.
(29)	Sakina	is	a nurse.
(30)	Prakash	is	in the library.
(31)	Ravi	was	downstairs.

A linking verb is a verb that functions as a linking device between the subject and the complement. The complement may be an adjective (sentences 26 and 27), a noun (sentences 28 and 29), a preposition phrase (sentence 30) or an adverb (sentence 31). In (28) the linking verb *been* is modified by the auxiliary verb *has*.

Exercise 3 (intermediate)

Arrange the following words under the order S + LV + CS. Remember to begin with a capital letter and end with a full stop.

1. were / busy / the boys.
   The boys (S) were (LV) busy. (CS)
2. winners / the Indians / were.
3. her brother / a fool lis
4. on Tuesday / the examination / will be
5. tall / my neighbour / is

6. is / at 4.30 / the meeting
7. right / may be / the policeman
8. is / her father / a doctor
9. a great leader / was / Lal Bahadur Shastri
10. Jane / talented / is
11. in the field / were / the boys
12. must have been / the party / enjoyable
13. upstairs / is / my mother
14. were / in the library / they
15. an architect / Manoj / is

There is a second category of linking verbs. These are verbs such as *appear, feel, look, seem, smell, sound, taste, become, get,* and *grow.*

	S	LV	CS
(32)	Mukesh	feels	happy.
(33)	This dog	seems	restless.
(34)	His aunt	became	a judge.
(35)	This will	remain	a secret.

Notice that verbs such as *appear, feel, look, seem, sound, taste, get* and *grow* may be followed by an adjective functioning as the subject complement. A few verbs such as *become, remain, seem* and *appear* may be followed by a noun phrase functioning as the subject complement.

Exercise 4 (intermediate)

Arrange the following words under the order S + LV + CS. Remember to begin with a capital letter and end with a full stop.

1. Amitabh / happy / appeared
2. strange / the music / sounded
3. feel / they / annoyed
4. a professor / my brother / became
5. Monisha / happy / looks
6. sad / seemed / Rekha
7. restless / this dog / seems
8. smells / the rose / sweet
9. bitter / this fruit / tastes
10. remained / he / the captain

Unit 2

SIMPLE SENTENCES 2

Read the following tables and the examples carefully and make as many meaningful sentences as possible from the tables.

TABLE 1

Example: *The soldiers saluted the captain.*

Subject	Transitive verb	Object
My sister The salesman The soldiers We The driver	saluted planted bought repaired sold	the car. the tyre. flowers. a doll. the captain.

TABLE 2

Example: *My mother cooks food in the evening.*

Subject	Transitive verb	Object	Adverbial
My mother	photographed	a letter	yesterday.
Our English teacher	met	a tiger	on Wednesday.
The man	cooks	an announcement	while we were attending his lecture.
Abhishek	wrote	food	
I	made	your sister	with his camera.

TABLE 3

Example: *Our teacher asked us a question.*

Subject	Transitive verb	Indirect object	Direct object
He	bought	John	her car.
Our aunt	gave	us	a question.
She	told	Rahul	a book.
Arun	asked	his daughter	a story.
Our teacher	offered	me	a present.

TABLE 4

Example: *The chief guest presented her a gold medal on the sports day.*

Subject	Transitive verb	Indirect object	Direct object	Adverbial
The chief guest	told	us	a dress	on her birthday.
Rita	bought	me	a gold medal	in the evening.
Our grandmother	presented	Meera	the book	on the sports day.
Her mother	sent	him	a story	yesterday.
The librarian	wrote	her	a letter	yesterday.

TABLE 5

Example: *The Board elected Rehman secretary.*

Subject	Transitive verb	Direct object	Object complement
She	found	the complaint	angry.
All of us	elected	Vinod	secretary.
The Board	consider	him	a genius.
His remark	called	Rehman	false.
The judge	made	her	a fool.

Pattern 3

Subject (S) + Transitive Verb (Trv) + Direct object (Od) + Adverbial (Adv)

- A transitive verb requires a direct object to complete it. A direct object is a pronoun or a noun.

	S	Trv	Od
(1)	Kapil Dev	hit	the ball.
(2)	Monica	has built	a house.

- A direct object can be an answer to *what* or *whom.*

(3)	He	addressed (whom)	the audience.
(4)	She	has read (what)	this novel.

- It is possible to use an adverbial with a transitive verb.

(5)	He	addressed	the audience	in the hall. (Adv)
(6)	She	has read	this novel	recently.

Exercise 1 (intermediate)

Arrange the following in the correct order. Remember to begin with a capital letter and end with a full stop. Mark elements of the rewritten sentences with the labels: S, Intrv, LV, Trv, CS, Od, Adv (if any).

1. my cycle / has taken / Shailaja
   Shailaja(S) has taken(Trv) my cycle (Od).
2. has been / ill / her father
   Her father (S) has been (LV) ill (CS).
3. a coat / I / need
4. is / warm / my coat
5. outside / your wife / is standing
6. the director / she / yesterday / met
7. every Sunday / visits / my friend / me
8. in the morning / she / slept
9. very pretty / your skirt / looks
10. have started / the game / they
11. a university professor / for five years / John / has been
12. boarded / she / the train / with her luggage
13. on Friday / the car / polished / the man
14. turned / sharply / the car
15. in the hall / the Principal / the speech / delivered
16. Rita / unhappy / at the party / looked

17. carried / his rifle / on his shoulder / the policeman
18. in Delhi / I / this book / bought
19. him / followed / everywhere / She
20. criticised / at the press conference / the government / the leader of the opposition

Pattern 4

Subject (S) + Transitive Verb (Trv) + Indirect Object (Oi) + Direct Object (Od) + Adverbial (Adv)

There is a group of verbs in English which require two objects, an indirect object, and a direct object.

	S	Trv	Oi	Od	(Adv)
(7)	He	gave	his daughter	a present	on her birthday.
(8)	Our aunt	told	us	a story.	
(9)	She	offered	me	her car.	
(10)	Arun	bought	John	a book	yesterday.
(11)	Our English teacher	asked	Meena	a question	during the quiz programme.

- The indirect object can be defined as the recipient of the action. The indirect object indicates *to whom* or *for whom* the action of the verb refers to.
- The indirect object can be a noun or a pronoun.
- The indirect object may often be replaced by a prepositional phrase beginning with *to* or *for*.

Exercise 2 (intermediate)

Arrange the following in the correct order. Remember to begin with a capital letter and end with a full stop. Mark elements of the rewritten sentences with the labels: S, Trv, Od, Oi (if any) and (Adv.) if any.

1. Delhi Public School / my daughter / attends
2. is weighing / the grocer / tea leaves
3. every night / us / a story / she / told
4. him / on Monday / granted / the Principal / leave
5. the ball / the goalkeeper / with his hands / caught
6. Mohit / difficult questions / asked / Seema / during the interview
7. recently / this house / I / have purchased

8. us / have paid / the rent / they
9. Mukesh / last month / this picture / painted
10. her car / has lent / me / Meenakshi
11. after we paid the money / us / gave / the receipt / the shop assistant
12. flowers / in the garden / planted / the gardener
13. us / teaches / English / Mr Kapoor
14. collected / we / our son's report card / in the morning
15. in the evening / Mrs Soni / tea / served / us

EXERCISE 3 (ELEMENTARY)

Replace the indirect object by a prepositional phrase in these sentences. Place the prepositional phrase at the most natural position.

1. My father gave me a book.
   My father gave a book to me.
2. Radha sent her brother a box of biscuits.
3. My mother bought me a bicycle.
4. Mr Sharma wrote us a letter.
5. He found her a house.
6. Shyam paid me the money.

Pattern 4a

Subject (S) + Transitive Verb (Trv) + Direct Object (Od) + to/ for + Noun or Pronoun (N) + Adverbial (Adv)

The indirect object can be used after the direct object with *to* or *for* used before it.

(12a) Sheila bought me a book. ✓
(12b) Sheila bought a book for me. ✓
(13a) She gave the boy a book. ✓
(13b) She gave a book to the boy. ✓

There are some verbs which cannot have an indirect object before the direct object, as we saw in Pattern 4.

(14a) She gave me the book. ✓
(14b) She gave the book to me. ✓
(15a) She explained me the situation. ✗
(15b) She explained the situation to me. ✓
(16a) Mohan reported me the matter. ✗
(16b) Mohan reported the matter to me. ✓

15a and 16a are unacceptable.

Verbs such as *admit, announce, declare, demonstrate, describe, explain, introduce, mention, propose, prove, repeat, report, suggest* etc. follow only pattern 4a.

EXERCISE 4 (INTERMEDIATE)

Write these sentences in the right order using the words in brackets. Sometimes more than one answer is possible. In that case, write all the answers.

1. We reported (the police / the matter).
   We reported the matter to the police.
2. Shabana introduced (me / her husband).
3. She admitted (her fault / her mother).
4. She suggested (me / it).
5. He confessed (the police / his crime).
6. You should not mention (anyone / it).
7. He declared (the Income Tax officer / his income).
8. Can you describe (us / your plan)?
9. You can tell (whatever you want / me).
10. He explained (the committee / his plan).

Pattern 5

Subject (S) + Transitive Verb (Trv) + Direct Object (Od) + Object Complement (Co) + Adverbial (Adv)

Some transitive verbs require a direct object to be followed by an object complement.

	S	Trv	Od	Co	Adv
(17)	The school	elected	Rakesh	Secretary	on Monday.
(18)	She	called	him	a fool.	
(19)	His remark	made	her	angry.	
(20)	The judge	found	the complaint	false.	

The object complement can be a noun/pronoun or an adjective.

EXERCISE 5 (INTERMEDIATE)

Arrange the following in the correct order. Remember to begin with a capital letter and end with a full stop. Mark elements of

the rewritten sentences with the labels: S, Intrv, LV, Trv, Cs, Co, Od, Oi, and (Adv).

1. our college captain / that girl / is
2. the potatoes / with a knife / Seema / sliced
3. made / her / they / the captain of the hockey team
4. was lying / the chair / in the centre
5. sour / has turned / the milk
6. with a key / she / the door / opened
7. us / our director / made / during the meeting / comfortable
8. her / called / Susie / her parents
9. the faculty / a watch / on her birthday / presented / her
10. a cycle / Rajesh / bought / his son
11. a dancer / for several years / has been / her sister
12. turned / on the bridge / the car / left
13. her / a house / they / built
14. considered / a success / the experiment / the Prime Minister
15. very impressive / that building / is
16. an army officer / her father / has been / for fifteen years
17. hit / my mother / the ball / with a stick
18. made / Varinder / the Principal / yesterday / the monitor of the class
19. at 2 o'clock / landed / at the Delhi airport / the plane
20. at the meeting / chose / they / Alka / their / leader

EXERCISE 6 (ADVANCED)

The functional labels for sentence patterns have been given below. Write two sentences for each of the sentence patterns.

1. S + Intrv
2. S + LV + Cs
3. S + Trv + Od
4. S + Trv + Oi + Od
5. S + Trv + Od + Co
6. S + Intrv + (Adv)
7. S + LV + Cs + (Adv)
8. S + Trv + Od + (Adv)
9. S + Trv + Oi + Od + (Adv)
10. S + Trv + Od + Co + (Adv)

EXERCISE 7 (ADVANCED)

Fill in the blanks with suitable words with the help of the hints given.

1. My brother .... (Trv) this building .... (Adv).
2. Sunita .... (LV) talented.
3. Arnaz wrote .... (Od) .... (Adv).
4. Our dog .... (Trv) .... (Od).
5. My father has been .... (Cs) for years.
6. We .... (Trv) the party immediately.
7. His father has planted .... (Od) in the garden.
8. The girls .... (Intrv. .... (Adv).
9. Samson .... (Intrv. .... (Adv) yesterday.
10. The car turned .... (Adv)
11. Samir called .... (Od) .... (Co).
12. Our English teacher considers .... (Od) .... (Co).
13. .... (S) chose Peter .... (Co) .... (Adv).
14. Madhuri looked .... (Cs) .... (Adv).
15. .... (S) .... (Trv) him intelligent.
16. Rakesh .... (Trv) Meera .... (Od) on her birthday.
17. Feroz and Sanjay .... (LV) policeman.
18. Mita and Kunal wrote .... (Adv).
19. .... (S) appears happy.
20. All of us consider him ....

Unit 3

COUNTABLE, UNCOUNTABLE AND PROPER NOUNS

Countable Nouns

Countable nouns are those nouns which have singular and plural forms. The singular form is used to refer to one person or thing, and the plural form is used to refer to more than one person or thing. For example:

boy – boys		man – men
book – books		child – children
car – cars		

So we can say *a boy, two toys, some boys, a car, five cars, ten weeks, a day* etc.

Exercise 1 (elementary)

Change the singular forms of the nouns to plural forms. Make necessary changes wherever required.

1. A lion is very powerful. *Lions are very powerful.*
2. A tree gives us shade. .... *give us shade.*
3. A cow is a domestic animal. .... *are domestic animals.*
4. A sparrow is a bird. .... *are birds.*
5. An aeroplane lands at an airport. .... *land at* ....
6. A mango is a delicious fruit. .... *are delicious* ....
7. A baby drinks milk.
8. A man or a woman can apply for this post.
9. A table and a chair can be made of wood.
10. A dog is a faithful animal.
11. A tiger runs fast.
12. A whale is a mammal.
13. A deer is very timid.
14. A train can go faster than a car.
15. An apple is good for health.
16. Monica keeps her car in her garage.
17. A fish lives in water.
18. An athlete needs good diet.

19. My brother visited my uncle yesterday.
20. The chemist sells medicines.
21. The policeman has caught the thief.
22. My sister is a pilot.
23. A pilot flies an aeroplane.
24. An author writes a novel.
25. A child likes playing.

Exercise 2 (elementary)

Change the plural forms of the nouns to singular forms. Make necessary changes wherever required.

1. My cousins are hockey players.
   My cousin is a hockey player.
2. Nightingales sing well.
   .... sings well.
3. We have two dogs and four ducks at home.
   We have a .... and a .... at home.
4. Children must drink milk.
   .... must drink milk.
5. Cars are made of steel.
   .... is made of steel.
6. There are jackals in this field.
   There is .... in this field.
7. Snakes can be dangerous.
   .... can be dangerous.
8. Eggs are good for health.
   .... is good for health.
9. Donkeys are animals.
   .... is an animal.
10. Tigers are ferocious.
    .... is ferocious.
11. Monkeys are intelligent.
    .... is intelligent.
12. I met two beautiful girls at the party.
    I met a .... at the party.
13. Birds fly in the sky.
    .... flies in the sky.

14. Lions are strong animals.
    .... is a strong animal.
15. Cauliflowers are tasty vegetables.
    .... is a tasty vegetable.
16. Doctors should be kind.
    .... should be kind.
17. Children must play in the evening.
    .... must play in the evening.
18. Army officers are very brave.
    .... is very brave.
19. Air hostesses look after the needs of passengers.
    .... looks after the needs of passengers.
20. Airforce pilots are very brave.
    .... is very brave.
21. Computers are used to send e-mail messages.
    .... is used to send e-mail messages.
22. Potatoes are vegetables.
    .... is a vegetable.
23. Policemen wear caps.
    .... wears a cap.
24. Horses are faithful animals.
    .... is a faithful animal.
25. Elephants are big animals.
    .... is a big animal.

Exercise 3 (elementary)

Fill in the blanks with either the singular or the plural form of the nouns in brackets.

1. My .... studies in class 7 (son).
2. My .... play their radio loudly (neighbour).
3. The .... that you bought me are lying on the table (book).
4. The .... is good for health (sunflower).
5. The .... are lying on the lawn (chair).
6. The .... whom you met at the station wants to see you (man).
7. The .... whose mother gave you a gift is waiting for you in the common room (girl).
8. The .... were kept in the fridge (apple).

9. The .... in the attic are nuisance (mouse).
10. The .... were waiting for you (child).

Uncountable Nouns

There are certain nouns which refer to general things like material, mass, a quality, or an abstract idea. Such nouns are called uncountable nouns. Uncountable nouns have only one form, i.e. the singular form. Usually, such nouns refer to metals, liquids, gases and certain other nouns.

metals	*liquids*	*gases*	*others*
gold	water	steam	sugar
silver	oil	air	sand
iron	milk	hydrogen	paper
aluminium	tea	oxygen	fire
copper	coffee	carbon	ice

(1) *Rubber* is used to make tyres.
(2) I need *some milk*.
(3) *Gold* is a precious metal.

Remember, we do not normally use *a/an* before an uncountable noun.

Exercise 4 (elementary)

Underline the noun(s) in each sentence and mention whether the underlined noun is a countable or an uncountable noun.

1. He is a fine actor. *countable*
2. I want some milk. *uncountable*
3. We need oil. ....
4. There are four cats ....
5. How much flour do you need? ....
6. We stayed in a hotel. ....
7. The bell is ringing. ....
8. We need to eradicate poverty. ....
9. The truth is that he didn't go anywhere. ....
10. I bought some coffee. ....
11. The keys are lying on the table. ....
12. She has read this book recently. ....
13. Education is necessary for our development. ....

14. History is an interesting subject. ....
15. We have bought some coal. ....
16. I have already bought some eggs. ....
17. She is a student. ....
18. We must perform our duty. ....
19. She lit the fire with a match. ....
20. Agriculture is very important for us. ....

Proper Nouns

Proper nouns are usually names of specific people, places, months, days, festivals etc. A proper noun always begins with a capital letter. Proper nouns do not take any articles before them.

- Personal names with or without titles:

Rakesh	Dr Kapoor	Col Srivastava
Madhu	Mr Johnson	President Clinton

- Names of festivals:

Diwali	Republic Day
Christmas	Independence Day

- Names of months, and days of the week:

January	Monday
December	Saturday

- Names of continents, countries, states, cities, towns etc.:

Europe	India	Maharashtra	Chandigarh
Asia	England	Haryana	Lucknow

However, there are some countries, states or cities before which the definite article *the* is used.

The Sudan   the Punjab   the Hague

- Names of lakes and mountains:

Salt Lake	Mount Everest
Lake Michigan	Mount Snowdon.

Exercise 5 (elementary)

Rewrite the following sentences using capital letters at the beginning of each proper noun.

1. We had a lot of fun on diwali last year.

2. delhi is the capital of india.
3. january is the first month of the year.
4. The prime minister visited lucknow on sunday.
5. I met mr sharma at the party in february.
6. During our visit to america, we went to see lake michigan.
7. asia is the largest continent.
8. I took rajesh to dr singh.
9. london is the capital of britain.
10. bill clinton was once the president of the u s a.
11. egypt is known for its pyramids.
12. We visited europe last year.
13. mohinder hit a century against pakistan.
14. All of us visited mr and mrs brown on christmas.
15. Mount everest is the highest mountain in the world.

Unit 4

COUNTABLE AND UNCOUNTABLE NOUNS

Forming countable plural nouns

- The most common way of forming a plural countable noun is by adding *-s* to the singular. For example:

  hen – hens pen – pens
  boy – boys son – sons

- *-es* is added to singular nouns that end in *-s*, *-z*, *-x*, *-sh* and *-ch*. For example:

  bus – buses church – churches
  box – boxes bush – bushes

- If a singular noun ends in a consonant (*t*, *r*, *d* etc.) + *y*, we add *-ies* to the plural changing *y* to *i*. For example:

  country – countries fairy – fairies
  lady – ladies city – cities

- If a singular noun ends in *-o*, we add *-es* to form a plural.

  potato – potatoes hero – heroes
  mango – mangoes buffalo – buffaloes

- If a singular noun ends in *-f* or *-fe*, *-f* is changed to *-v* and we add *-es* after *-v*. For example:

  wife – wives knife – knives
  wolf – wolves life – lives

- Some other singular nouns ending in *-f* have only *-s* added to the plural form. For example :

  roof – roofs proof – proofs
  handkerchief – handkerchiefs chief – chiefs

- In some cases, the plural is formed by changing the vowel. For example:

  foot – feet man – men
  goose – geese tooth – teeth

- Two nouns have *-en* or *-ren* added to the plural form.

  ox – oxen child – children

- Some nouns have the same singular and plural forms.

  cattle – cattle aircraft – aircraft

  sheep – sheep

Exercise 1 (elementary)

Give the plural forms of the following singular nouns.

1. woman
2. scarf
3. dwarf
4. watch
5. torch
6. dress
7. deer
8. leaf
9. fly
10. city
11. tigress
12. cargo
13. mattress
14. inch
15. fox
16. box
17. bush
18. loaf
19. country
20. mice
21. goose
22. mosquito
23. monkey
24. factory

Exercise 2 (elementary)

Rewrite the following sentences using the plural forms of the countable nouns. Make necessary changes wherever required.

1. The book is in the bag.
2. I bought a torch yesterday.
3. We saw an ox on the way.
4. We need a leaf for our practical class.
5. There is a knife lying on the table.
6. We saw a deer in the zoo.
7. That calf is very young.
8. The thief was very cunning.
9. A tomato always turns red.
10. A hero always loves his country.
11. A child is playing outside.
12. I wanted a scarf.
13. She saw an aeroplane in the sky.
14. There is a fish in the water.
15. She bought a dress yesterday.

EXERCISE 3 (ELEMENTARY)

Change the following singular nouns into plural nouns.

1. a tailor; many ....
2. a man; five ....
3. one bag; several ....
4. a tap; ten ....
5. an aircraft; many ....
6. a woman; seven ....
7. the tree; the ....
8. the table; twenty ....
9. a coat; many ....
10. a lady; several ....
11. a church; the ....
12. a horse; six ....
13. the clock; the ....
14. one doctor; three ....
15. a knife; many ....
16. a handkerchief; fifteen ....
17. a pilot; several ....
18. the pen; thirty ....
19. a child; several ....
20. a book; many ....
21. one bottle; several ....
22. a mango; several ....
23. the crow; two ....
24. a sheep; many ....
25. an officer; several ....

Examples of uncountable nouns

There are uncountable nouns, which refer to general things like qualities and processes rather than to individual items or events.

agriculture	duty	happiness	money	time
anger	education	health	music	wealth
beauty	faith	labour	poverty	wind
courage	fashion	love	power	work
death	fear	mercy	sleep	youth

(1) *Agriculture* is important for the growth of a country.
(2) *Courage* does not require *strength*.

The uncountable nouns cannot have *a/an* in front of them. They cannot be changed into their plural forms.

(3) I'd like *some water* (not *a water*).
(4) It is *our duty* to help you (not *our duties*).

Quantifying uncountable nouns

We can use expressions of quantity such as *piece, item, slice* before uncountable nouns to quantify them.

a drop of water	a gallon of water	three cups of tea
a cup of tea	a piece of cake	five loaves of bread
a loaf of bread	a pinch of salt	two bottles of milk
a bottle of milk	a piece of paper	ten kilos of flour
a kilo of flour	a litre of oil	six litres of oil

EXERCISE 4 (ADVANCED)

Fill in the blanks by using words from the following boxes. Make as many sentences as you want to.

a	cup piece jar bottle bar glass	of	coffee juice paper tea luggage chocolate cake ink milk honey

1. I gave her ....
2. I bought .... yesterday.
3. I need ....
4. There is .... lying on the table.
5. She lost ....
6. Can you get me .... ?
7. She wants ....
8. He drinks ....
9. Can you give me .... ?
10. Would you have .... ?

EXERCISE 5 (ADVANCED)

Use the noun given in brackets with *a/an + singular noun* if it is a countable noun, *or an expression of quantity* if it is an uncountable noun.

1. I met .... yesterday (smart boy).

   I met a smart boy yesterday.
2. I requested her to give me .... (water).

   I requested her to give me a glass of water.
3. I bought .... from the corner shop (bread).
4. She gave me .... yesterday (pot).
5. Radha wants .... (milk).
6. There is .... lying on the floor (pen).
7. There is .... lying on the floor (paper).
8. My mother gave my sister .... at breakfast (cake).
9. My mother gave my sister .... at breakfast (apple).
10. Tom brought home .... last night (dog).
11. Rasheeda wanted .... (tea).
12. My father planted .... in our house (tree).
13. He put .... in his scooter (oil).
14. She bought .... yesterday (jam).
15. She bought .... yesterday (book).

Unit 5

POSSESSIVE, GENDER AND COLLECTIVE NOUNS

Noun Possessive

We show possession in English by using the possessive form of a noun.

- We use the apostrophe + s ('s) for possessives after the nouns that refer to *people, animals* and after *proper nouns.*
  (1) I like my *father's house.*
  (2) He pulled the *dog's ear.*
  (3) That is *Shefali's camera.*
- We add only the apostrophe ('s) if the plural noun ends in *-s.*
  (4) Mr Bhalla constructed my *brothers' house.*
  (5) He was cleaning the *soldiers' guns.*
- We add the apostrophe (') if the plural noun does not end in *-s.*
  (6) She pulled *the oxen's tails.*
  (7) *The men's shirts* are lying in the corner.

Exercise 1 (elementary)

Write down the correct possessive forms of the following phrases.

1. the ear of the cat
   the cat's ear
2. the shop belonging to the grocer
   the grocer's shop
3. the house owned by Mary
4. the car owned by Salman
5. the paw of the cat
6. the plays of Shakespeare
7. the book belonging to Sushma
8. the purse held by Menaka
9. the plane owned by Mr Tata
10. the legs of the lions
11. the factory owned by Dr Kapoor
12. the eyes of the elephants

13. the cycles of the boys
14. the marriage of Lekha
15. the toys belonging to the children
16. the frocks of the girls
17. the room of the teachers
18. the saris of the women
19. the coats of the ladies
20. the friend of my brother

- We do not use apostrophe + s (– *'s*) after nouns that name *things*, *a place*, etc. We use *of* with these nouns.

    (8) Delhi is *the capital of India.* (not *India's capital*)
    (9) *The end of this book* is very interesting.

Exercise 2 (intermediate)

Complete the following sentences with the help of the words within brackets.

1. I was sitting in .... (the front / the place)
   I was sitting in the front of the place.
2. Swati needs .... (scooter / your mother)
   Swati needs your mother's scooter.
3. What is .... ? (the name / this theatre)
4. Where is .... ? (the car / your brother)
5. We liked .... (the beginning / the movie)
6. I liked .... (the speech / President)
7. The Principal gave me .... (the book / Maria)
8. .... is a doctor (the father / Manoj)
9. Paris .... (the capital / France)
10. .... are at the back. (the seats / the men)
11. The child was playing with .... (the tail / the cat)
12. Early morning is .... (the best part / the day)
13. What is .... ? (the meaning / this word)
14. We are afraid of .... (the roar / the lion)
15. She is .... (the sister / Elizabeth)
16. .... is very strong. (the roof / the house)
17. We've kept .... in the corner. (the bags / the students)
18. .... are kept in the corner. (the books / the children)
19. .... is very attractive. (the colour / your car)
20. .... were built in 1985. (the houses / my brothers)

MASCULINE AND FEMININE NOUNS

Some nouns in English have distinct masculine and feminine forms and thus they may be referred to by the pronouns *he* or *she*.

(10) I met a *boy* yesterday on the road. *He* asked me if I could help him cross the road.

(11) There is a *girl* outside the classroom. *She* wants to talk to you.

Such nouns have contrasting masculine and feminine forms.

son – daughter	father – mother	bull – cow
husband – wife	nephew – niece	cock – hen

There is a group of nouns which has contrasting masculine and feminine forms but the feminine form can be formed by adding *-ess* to the masculine form.

host – hostess	prince – princess	lion – lioness
waiter – waitress	god – goddess	tiger – tigress

EXERCISE 3 (ELEMENTARY)

Rewrite the following sentences changing the gender of the underlined words. Make necessary changes in the underlined pronouns also.

1. My father is a doctor. He goes to his clinic at 8 o' clock in the morning.
   My mother is a doctor. She goes to her clinic at 8 o' clock in the morning.
2. I met your uncle at the party last night. He was looking very healthy.
3. We saw a lioness in the circus. It looked very ferocious.
4. Rakesh met the Queen of Spain at the Government House. She has invited him to Spain.
5. The bridegroom looked very happy. He was accompanied by his brothers.
6. That man is a policeman. He lives in Gomti Nagar.
7. You've met my brothers. All of them live with my father.
8. We've bought five cows. We have brought them from Haryana.
9. His mother-in-law is a professor. She teaches in the English department.
10. His daughters have joined the army. They are undergoing training in Chennai.

EXERCISE 4 (INTERMEDIATE)

The underlined words here are in a particular gender. Fill in the blanks with the gender which is the opposite of the underlined words.

1. My *father* is a police officer and my *mother* is a doctor.
2. My niece is in class 3 and my .... is in class 1.
3. My brother goes to school at 7 o' clock and my .... goes to school at 8 o'clock in the morning.
4. My .... is a nurse and my uncle is a doctor.
5. Shah Rukh Khan is the hero and Karisma is the .... of the film.
6. Rakesh and Seema acted as prince and .... in the play.
7. Mukesh has been a .... and Rekha has been a widow for five years now.
8. We went to the zoo and saw lions and .... in the cage.
9. My brother owns a big farm, where he has kept several cows and ....
10. The tigress was running after the deer but the .... was sitting under the tree.
11. We met the bride and the .... at the reception.
12. Your stallion and .... looked very smart at the horse show.
13. His son is a college lecturer and his .... is a schoolteacher.
14. Amitabh is an actor and Meenakshi is an ....
15. Lord Rama was a .... and Sita was his queen.
16. Rajesh and Rekha work as waiter and .... in a restaurant.
17. Mukesh and Vaishali are fifty-year-olds and have not got married. He is a bachelor and she is a ....
18. They have kept two cocks and ten .... in the backyard of their house.
19. Her mother-in-law works in a bank and her .... works in a company.
20. The count and the .... were sitting in the corner during the party.

NOUNS WITH NEUTER GENDER

There is a large class of nouns in the neuter gender which can be referred to by *he / she* depending upon the sex of the person: *adult, child, cousin, doctor, foreigner, friend, journalist, lawyer, lecturer, musician, officer, professor, passenger, reader, scientist, singer, teacher, typist, writer,* etc.

(12a) I met *my doctor* yesterday. *He* asked me to see *him* on Monday.

(12b) I met *my doctor* yesterday. *She* asked me to see *her* on Monday.

Exercise 5 (intermediate)

Fill in the blanks with either *he* or *she*.

1. My cousin is a doctor. .... gets up at 6 o'clock in the morning and makes breakfast for her husband and children.
2. Mr Singh is a brilliant lawyer. .... has three junior lawyers working with him.
3. Mrs Kapoor is our English teacher. .... teaches us English grammar.
4. Asha is a great singer. .... has sung thousands of songs.
5. The writer of this book is quite young. .... wrote her first novel when she was only eighteen years old.
6. Our English professor told us to read at least two novels. .... has been teaching Dickens to his students for the last ten years.
7. There was a visitor looking for you. .... has left her visiting card for you.
8. Rajan works as a musician in Big India Ltd. .... has worked in this company for the last five years.
9. Rakhi was my Ph.D. student. .... finished her research in two years.
10. The cook will not come today. .... daughter informed me that he was down with fever.
11. Mr Prakash has been a journalist for fifteen years. .... articles are rated very high by the people.
12. Your guest has left. By mistake, ... has forgotten her spectacles here.
13. My son is a student and .... is very good in English.
14. My daughter is a student and .... is very good in maths.
15. My lawyer has told me that .... would inform me as soon as she gets a copy of the judgement.

Collective Nouns

There are certain nouns like *government, board, army* which can be treated both as singular or plural nouns. Collective nouns can be followed by either singular or plural verbs.

(13a) The team has been practising for the last one month.
(13b) The team have been practising for the last one month.

Some more examples of collective nouns are: *army, family, committee, group, community, press, herd, staff, club, public.*

There are some collective nouns which have singular forms but are followed by plural verbs. This means they have singular forms but have plural sense. For example, *police, people, military, cattle.*

(14) *The police are looking* into the matter.
(15) There *are many people* at the party.

Exercise 6 (advanced)

Fill in the blanks with *is, are, has,* or *have.* Wherever possible use both *is* and *are* or *has* and *have.*

1. The company .... given a twenty per cent bonus to all its employees.
2. The police .... trying to contact the Chief Minister.
3. The military .... practising these days for the Republic Day Parade.
4. The government .... decided to raise the monthly scholarship of all the students.
5. There .... many people in the hall.
6. The Indian cricket team .... made 416 runs in the first innings.
7. The staff .... decided to take the tutorials in the afternoon.
8. The board .... discussing your proposal.
9. The committee .... meeting tomorrow to discuss your proposal.
10. The public .... blocked all the entrance gates.
11. A lot of people .... appealed to the President.
12. The army .... advancing towards the border.
13. The public .... happy with the decrease in the oil prices.
14. The press .... an important institution in democracy.
15. There .... many people at the party.

Nouns with Plural Forms only

There are certain nouns referring to clothes and tools which are usually used in the plural forms. For example, *scissors, trousers, glasses, belongings, jeans, pyjamas, binoculars, shorts, knickers,* etc.

(16) He always wears *blue trousers.*
(17) *Those jeans* are very good.

These nouns can combine with *a pair of,* (three) *pairs of.*

(18) I bought a *pair of jeans* yesterday.

Exercise 7 (elementary)

Use *a pair of* before the *noun* within brackets.

1. *I need a pair of glasses. (glasses)*
2. She gave me .... for my birthday. (trousers)
3. Where can I buy .... ? (scissors)
4. We should have bought .... (binoculars)
5. You must keep .... with you. (pliers)
6. She wants .... (tights)
7. She bought .... on Monday. (spectacles)
8. You need .... (shorts)
9. She requires .... (forceps)
10. I bought .... yesterday. (laces)

Exercise 8 (advanced)

Fill in the blanks with appropriate words.

1. Those trousers .... good.
2. Where .... my glasses?
3. How much did you pay for your pyjamas? .... look very expensive.
4. Your jeans .... new.
5. Her new glasses .... made of plastic lenses.
6. Your trousers .... lying on your bed.
7. The clothes .... been ironed well.
8. Are you looking for the scissors? It .... lying on the table.
9. His shorts .... rather worn out.
10. Your knickers .... been given to the tailor.

Unit 6

ARTICLES

THE INDEFINITE ARTICLE: A/AN

A/an is used before a countable singular noun. We use *a* in front of a word that begins with a consonant sound and *an* in front of a word that begins with a vowel sound.

a church	*an apple*
a man	*an officer*
a big shoe	*an interesting book*
a book	*an eye*
a tall girl	*an old man*

EXERCISE 1 (ELEMENTARY)

Use *a* or *an* before each of these noun phrases.

1. .... long train
2. .... airy room
3. .... table
4. .... ass
5. .... beautiful flower
6. .... ideal house
7. .... factory
8. .... old factory
9. .... very old factory
10. .... well decorated hall
11. .... extremely cold winter
12. .... very old man
13. .... man
14. .... bicycle
15. .... inkpot
16. .... umbrella
17. .... iron gate
18. .... brass gate
19. .... expensive coat
20. .... cat

- We use *a/an* with a singular countable noun when we talk about the noun in a general sense.
  (1) *A dog* is a domestic animal. (all dogs in general)
  (2) *An air conditioner* can be of great help in summer. (all air conditioners in general)
- We can also use the plural form of the countable noun when we talk about the noun in a general sense.
  (3) *Dogs* are domestic animals. (all dogs in general)
  (4) *Air conditioners* can be of great help in summer. (all air conditioners in general)

EXERCISE 2 (ELEMENTARY)

Rewrite the following sentences using the singular forms of the nouns. Make necessary changes wherever required.

1. Young dogs are very playful.
2. Old men can be active.
3. Men are mortal.
4. Leaves are green.
5. Bank officers work very hard.
6. Compact discs are very expensive.
7. Horses are faithful animals.
8. Apples are good for health.
9. Students wear uniforms.
10. Old computers are quite cheap.
11. Red roses look very beautiful.
12. Chairs have four legs.
13. Oranges taste good.
14. Old houses have big rooms.
15. Policemen wear caps.
16. Ducks are birds.
17. Lions are big animals.
18. Elephants have big bodies.
19. Old novels can be educative books.
20. Cheap watches do not last long.

EXERCISE 3 (ELEMENTARY)

Rewrite the following sentences using the plural forms of the nouns. Make necessary changes, wherever required.

1. A politician should be sincere.
2. A hen is a bird.
3. An orange is a delicious fruit.
4. A mouse is afraid of a cat.
5. A jet aeroplane flies fast.
6. A child needs to drink milk.
7. A cauliflower is a vegetable.
8. A computer can solve a problem quickly.
9. A cricket player should have good health.
10. A mango tree gives us shade.
11. A big town sometimes is better than a city.
12. A train runs faster than a bus.
13. A railway platform is a busy place.

14. A student should work hard.
15. An FM radio has excellent reception.

- We use *a/an* before singular countable nouns, when we use them to describe people or things.
  - (5) She is *a teacher.*
  - (6) Mukesh is *an army officer.*
  - (7) It is *a tiger.*
- We can also use an adjective + noun pattern.
  - (8) She is *a good teacher.*
  - (9) Rita is *a tall girl.*
- We can also use *a/an* before the nationality words used as nouns.
  - (10) Mukesh is *an Indian.*
  - (11) Edward is *an American.*

Exercise 4 (elementary)

Answer the following questions using the nouns within brackets after *a/an*.

1. What is Rakesh? (pilot) *Rakesh is a pilot.*
2. What is she? (cook)
3. What is it? (tree)
4. What is it? (glass table)
5. What is Diana? (beautiful model)
6. Who is he? (German)
7. Who is she? (Canadian)
8. What is he? (IAS officer)
9. What is it? (excellent book)
10. What is he? (good doctor)
11. Who is she? (Australian)
12. Who is he? (Chinese)
13. What is it? (ant)
14. What is Shefali? (university lecturer)
15. What is Varinder? (student)
16. What is it? (giant panda)
17. Who is he? (Austrian)
18. What is she? (nurse)
19. What is he? (cricket player)
20. What is it? (folding chair)

- We usually use *a/an* when we mention someone or something for the first time. When the noun refers to the person or thing already mentioned, *the* is used.
  - (12) I met *a man* and *a woman* at the party yesterday. *The man* was wearing a *formal suit* but the woman was wearing a *salwar-kameez*.
  - (13) We've killed *a wolf.* *The wolf* killed a shepherd boy last week.
  - (14) She was eating *an apple.* *The apple* was brought from Shimla.

Exercise 5 (intermediate)

Fill in the blanks with *a/an* or *the*.

1. She has made .... painting for you. You can keep .... painting in your house.
2. .... man and .... woman are waiting for you outside. .... woman is quite tall.
3. .... man walked into .... bank in Lucknow and gave .... cheque to the cashier. .... cashier looked at .... cheque and returned it to .... man.
4. Rahul: Is there .... chair to sit on?
   Meera: You can sit on .... stool there.
5. She killed .... wolf last week. .... wolf had been roaming around the village for several days.
6. She was writing .... letter, when I visited her. After writing .... letter, she gave it to her servant.
7. She delivered .... lecture on Shakespeare on Monday. Everyone liked .... lecture.
8. I've kept .... egg for you on the table. You can eat .... egg in the evening.
9. I saw .... car coming in the opposite direction. .... car stopped as it reached the grocer's shop.
10. There was .... aeroplane landing at the airport. However, ... aeroplane took .... turn before it landed.

Exercise 6 (intermediate)

Fill in the blanks with *some, a/an,* or *the*. Some of the blanks do not require any of these words.

1. I'd like .... butter, please.

2. The government has decided to impart .... free education.
3. .... democracy has been successful in our country.
4. She bought .... sugar yesterday.
5. My mother bought .... pen for me yesterday.
6. .... religion teaches us .... love for .... mankind.
7. Let's listen to .... music.
8. I wrote .... letter in the morning.
9. I've finished .... homework.
10. Karishma is suffering from .... flu.
11. India wants .... peace with her neighbours.
12. I'd like .... apple, please.
13. I need .... new coat.
14. She needs .... cloth to make .... shirt.
15. Would you like .... tea?
16. Would you like .... piece of cake?
17. There are .... biscuits lying on the table.
18. We have .... house in .... Hyderabad.
19. She cooks .... dinner in .... evening.
20. You may put .... butter on .... slice.

EXERCISE 7 (ADVANCED)

Fill in the blanks with *a/an* or *the*.

There was .... knock on my door at 2 o'clock in the morning. I opened .... door and found .... old man standing at .... door. He had .... gun in his hand and .... cigarette in his mouth. I didn't realise that there was .... young man behind him. .... old man pointed .... pistol at me and .... young man took out .... piece of paper. He gave .... piece of paper to me. I read it and realised that it was .... arrest warrant to arrest one Mr Kalra. I told them that I was not Kalra and that they had come to the wrong house. .... old man put .... pistol in his pocket and .... young man took back .... arrest warrant from me. Both of them apologised to me and left my house.

Unit 7

THE DEFINITE ARTICLE AND THE ZERO ARTICLE

THE DEFINITE ARTICLE: THE

- *The* is used before those nouns which refer to only one *person, thing,* or *group.* Sometimes, this can be due to the situational reference.

    (1) *The earth* revolves around *the sun.*
    (2) Can I see *the manager*? (at a bank)
    (3) The *monsoon* has arrived earlier this year.
    (4) *The President* is visiting Mumbai on Tuesday. (of India)

- *The* is used before a noun which has become definite because it has been mentioned a second time. In other words, the noun has a back reference.

    (5) She bought a bus and a taxi last month. She has got the license to run *the bus* on the Delhi–Kanpur route and she has given *the taxi* to her son to run it as a local taxi.

- *The* is also used before a noun which has been identified or made unique, because it has been modified by a relative clause or a phrase following it.

    (6) *The man who is standing under the tree* wants to meet you.
    (7) *The dog barking over there* is ferocious.
    (8) *The man in the red shirt* is a preacher.

- *The* is used with superlatives and *first, second* etc. used as modifiers of the noun.

    (9) Shikha is *the best student* in our class.
    (10) Charles was *the first person* to board the plane.

- *The* is also used before words referring to nationality.

    (11) *The Indians* have contributed a lot to the development of IT.
    (12) *The Americans* are very hardworking.

- We often use *the* before the names of *organisations, newspapers, hotels, restaurants, theatres, cinema halls, oceans* etc.

the United Nations
the Times of India
the Atlantic Ocean
the Oberoi Sheraton
the Globe

Exercise 1 (elementary)

Use *the* wherever necessary.

1. moon revolves around the earth.
2. table lying in corner was made by my grandfather.
3. Germans have developed the automobile industry.
4. Diana is most punctual woman in our office.
5. I read Hindustan Times in the morning.
6. My mother brought a dog last week but my father did not like dog and gave it to our neighbours.
7. I need to see Principal.
8. We went to see a play at Prithvi theatre yesterday.
9. Rekha is tallest girl in our class.
10. You can take book with blue cover.
11. sun is shining.
12. I visited Shimla last year and stayed in house, where I was born.
13. next meeting of Board of Directors will be held in Taj Palace Hotel.
14. Japanese can be very friendly.
15. Prime Minister will visit Chandigarh next month.
16. There is a boy and some girls in the hall. boy is playing with a ball and girls are playing badminton.
17. lady in red dress is a police officer.
18. Canadians are good in playing hockey.
19. We stayed at Clark Avadh, when we visited Lucknow last month.
20. Vinay is second man to win this contest.

The Zero Article

We do not use any article

- when a plural countable noun is used in a generic or general sense.
  - (13) *Tigers* can run very fast.
  - (14) *Mangoes* are in great demand in the west.
- when uncountable nouns are used in a generic sense.
  - (15) *Water* is necessary for our survival.
  - (16) *Oil* is used for frying.

- before proper nouns.

  (17) I met *Hussein* yesterday.

- before the names of countries, cities, towns and villages.

  (18) *India* has liberalised its economy.
  (19) *Ujjain* is an ancient city.

- before nouns such as *school, hospital, bed, church, class, college, university, work.*

  (20) She goes to *college* in the morning.
  (21) I went to *bed* at 10 pm last night.

- before means of transport such as *by air, by bus, by car, by land, by sea, by ship, by train.*

  (22) We went to Goa *by bus.*
  (23) I always travel *by train.*

EXERCISE 2 (INTERMEDIATE)

Fill in the blanks with *a/an*, if necessary. Some blanks do not require any article (zero-article).

1. Suresh's father is .... teacher. He goes to .... school at 8 am by .... bus.
2. I saw .... cat yesterday. It was carrying .... rat in its mouth.
3. He met with .... accident last week. He is still in .... hospital.
4. We bought .... house last year. It is made of .... wood .... cement and .... plaster.
5. .... smoking is injurious to health. Therefore, our country should not allow .... production of .... cigarettes.
6. .... mangoes grow in abundance in .... India and .... apples grow in abundance in .... Australia.
7. We will go by .... train and my sister will go by .... bus to Delhi.
8. .... air is .... essential element for .... life on .... earth.
9. .... rain is good for .... agriculture but .... excessive rain can cause .... floods.
10. .... wood is used for building .... houses and making .... furniture.
11. My father is .... bank officer. He goes to .... bank at 9 o'clock in the morning.
12. .... Venkat is going to build .... factory in .... Hyderabad. He is getting .... cement from .... Kanpur and .... steel from .... Tata Nagar.

13. He is .... vegetarian. He does not eat .... meat.
14. Farida can drive .... car but she goes to .... work by .... bus.
15. He drinks .... milk at breakfast.
16. .... gold is .... precious metal.
17. Do you want .... sugar in your tea?
18. They went to .... Chennai by .... train.
19. She goes to .... office at 8 o'clock in the morning.
20. He went by .... air to Delhi and then took .... train to .... Chandigarh.
21. .... computers have .... important role to play in .... education.
22. My brother bought .... sugar, ... oil and .... salt yesterday and my sister-in-law bought .... shirt and .... pen for my sister.
23. We went by .... air to Hyderabad.
24. Rajneesh and his friends play .... cricket everyday. Each boy has .... cricket ball and .... cricket bat. They play .... cricket at .... school and sometimes at .... home.
25. Vinod is .... army officer. He goes to .... office by .... car. He comes .... home in the evening.

Exercise 3 (advanced)

Fill in the blanks with *a/an* or *the*, if necessary. Some blanks do not require any article.

1. I took my children to the zoo on Sunday. We saw .... tiger and .... panther in .... zoo and .... tiger seemed to be very young and ferocious but .... panther was old and looked harmless.
2. Nita's father was .... engineer. He worked for .... construction company. .... company was owned by .... Russian.
3. We couldn't see .... road in front of us. Therefore, we parked .... car on .... side of .... road and waited for .... clear weather to set in.
4. .... tea can be very refreshing in .... evening. I often have .... friends come over for .... cup of tea and .... pleasant chat.
5. You must buy .... refrigerator because it is .... necessity these days.
6. She hired .... taxi to visit .... Amritsar.
7. Mahesh bought .... scooter and .... car last year. But as he is in need of money, he wants to sell .... car.

8. She hit him on .... head.
9. .... Prime Minister is visiting Jammu next Monday and therefore, ... Chief Minister wants to have .... meeting of all .... secretaries.
10. .... oil is essential for .... industrial development of .... country.
11. Her father has been .... judge for nine years. He goes to .... court at nine in the morning.
12. .... Rakesh and .... Meera are .... engineers. They work in .... construction company.
13. We met .... pilot and .... air hostess at .... cinema yesterday.
14. There is .... book lying on .... table.
15. .... Governor will visit .... Nainital tomorrow. He will be received by .... Chief Minister at .... boat club.
16. She wants to marry .... doctor.
17. It is a fact that .... earth is round.
18. .... girl wearing .... red coat is my cousin.
19. .... jacket lying in .... corner is made of .... leather.
20. Manish is .... richest man in our town.
21. She was .... first student to join this college.
22. .... *Indian Express* is .... interesting paper.
23. .... French are very proud of their language.
24. We went to .... college by .... bus.
25. You need .... flour, ... eggs and .... sugar to bake .... cake.
26. We crossed .... Atlantic Ocean at night.
27. .... elephants are found in .... South Asia.
28. Sushila was sent to .... prison on .... charge of stealing .... car.
29. We went to .... Aden by .... ship. .... ship in which we travelled was called .... Emperor Akbar.
30. .... potatoes can be added to any curry.

Unit 8

SOME, ANY, A LOT OF, (A) LITTLE, (A) FEW

Some and Any

As a general rule *some* and *any* are used before plural nouns or uncountable nouns.

(1) I want *some potatoes*.
(2) I want *some milk*.
(3) I don't want *any potatoes*.

Remember the following basic rules:

- Use *some* in positive sentences.

    (4) I'm going to buy *some vegetables*.
    (5) There is *some ice* in the fridge.

- Use *any* in negative sentences.

    (6) I'm not going to buy *any vegetables*.
    (7) There isn't *any ice* in the fridge.

- With questions beginning with *is, are, was, were*, we may usually use *any*.

    (8) Are there *any eggs* in the basket?
    (9) Is there *any water* in the jug?

- With questions beginning with *would you like* or *do you want, can I have*, we may usually use *some*.

    (10) Would you like *some tea*, please?
    (11) Do you want *some eggs*?

Exercise 1 (intermediate)

Fill in the blanks with *some* or *any*.

1. There are .... apples lying on the table.
2. There is .... juice in the cup.
3. There is .... water in the jug but there aren't .... glasses.
4. There isn't .... oil in the bottle.
5. I'll pay the bill. I have .... money in my pocket.
6. I can't pay the bill. I don't have .... money in my pocket.
7. I'm going to the market to buy .... mangoes.

8. I'm not going to buy .... vegetables.
9. Is there .... soup in the bowl?
10. Would you like to eat .... meat tonight?
11. We have .... butter but we don't have .... bread.
12. I want to wash my hands. Is there .... soap?
13. I am very hungry. Can I have .... chicken, please?
14. I don't have .... stamps.
15. I want .... oranges.
16. I want .... milk.
17. I don't have .... pens left in the box.
18. We had .... orange juice in the morning and therefore, we couldn't drink .... juice in the afternoon.
19. Would you like to have .... chocolate?
20. Please have .... biscuits.
21. I can't eat .... carrots, but I can have .... meat.
22. Is there .... sauce in the bottle?
23. She has .... very interesting music cassettes.
24. I don't want .... jam at breakfast, but can I have .... milk?
25. There isn't .... tea in the pan.

SOME / ANY + BODY / ONE / THING / WHERE

For people we may use *somebody, someone, anybody* or *anyone.* For things we may use *something* or *anything* and for places we may use *somewhere* or *anywhere.*

- We use *somebody, someone, sometime,* and *somewhere* in positive sentences.

  (12) There is *somebody / someone* near the window.
  (13) I've got *something* in my pocket.
  (14) I kept my keys *somewhere.*

- We use *anybody, anyone, anything, anywhere* in negative sentences.

  (15) I didn't meet *anybody / anyone* in office today.
  (16) There isn't *anything* in the cupboard.
  (17) We aren't going *anywhere* today.

- We usually use *anybody, anyone, anything* or *anywhere* in questions.

  (18) Is there *anybody / anyone* in the house?

(19) Are you going *anywhere* today?

- We usually use *somebody / someone, something* and *somewhere* in questions when we expect 'yes' as the answer to the questions. We also use these with offers and requests beginning *would you like...*

(20) Was there *something* you wanted to have with tea?

(21) Would you like to go *somewhere*?

Exercise 2 (intermediate)

Fill in the blanks with *somebody, someone, something, somewhere, anybody, anyone, anything* or *anywhere* in the following sentences.

1. I want .... to clean my house.
2. I've kept .... in your bag.
3. We didn't go .... last summer.
4. It's dark outside. I can't see ....
5. Would you like .... to eat?
6. She didn't eat .... at lunch.
7. I can't see .... sitting in the room.
8. Your cycle must be lying .... in the garden.
9. Did you meet .... at the station?
10. She looks very sad today. Is there .... wrong with her?
11. Do you want to buy .... in this shop?
12. He said .... but I couldn't understand him.
13. They live .... on the outskirts of Delhi.
14. Are you going .... tonight?
15. Do you know .... about cricket?

Exercise 3 (advanced)

Fill in the blanks with *some, any, somebody, someone, something, somewhere, anybody, anyone, anything* or *anywhere* in the following sentences.

1. Can I have .... sugar in my tea?
2. There are .... mangoes lying in the fridge.
3. He didn't say .... to Sadhana.
4. I want to buy .... shirts but I don't have .... money.
5. Would you like to have .... with the soup?
6. We didn't buy .... milk last week.
7. She had .... juice in the morning.

8. Can you give me .... information about your college?
9. She has left her luggage .... and now she can't find it .... in the airport.
10. You can stay .... you want to.
11. I can't find .... ice in the fridge.
12. Is there .... in your class who can speak German?
13. Does .... want more ice cream?
14. I've not read .... of these books, but my brother has read .... of them.
15. There is .... wood lying in the corner. You can take .... for tomorrow's exhibition.
16. I hope you meet .... at the station.
17. We haven't bought .... fans recently.
18. Are you cooking .... vegetables for dinner?
19. She didn't say .... to ....
20. We'll burst .... crackers during his wedding.

MUCH, MANY, A LOT OF

- A *lot of* can be used with *uncountable* or *plural nouns*. For example, *a lot of water, a lot of money, a lot of people, a lot of books*.

  (22) I drank *a lot of water*.
  (23) There were *a lot of people* at the meeting.

- *Much* is used with uncountable nouns. For example, *much time, much tea, much milk, much money*. *Much* is usually used in negative sentences and questions.

  (24) There isn't *much milk* in the bottle.
  (25) Is there *much money* left in your account?

- *Many* is used with plural nouns. For example, *many people, many books, many friends, many dogs*. *Many* is usually used in negative sentences and questions.

  (26) They don't have *many books*.
  (27) Do you have *many friends*?

EXERCISE 4 (ADVANCED)

Fill in the blanks with *a lot of, much* or *many*.

1. I couldn't meet .... people, when I visited Shimla last month.

2. You must drive fast. We don't have .... time to catch the train.
3. Sarika drinks .... juice everyday.
4. Do you have .... books in your library?
5. She bought .... antiques at the auction.
6. There are .... trees around our house.
7. Why have you kept .... horses in your farm?
8. She can't speak German fluently. She makes .... mistakes.
9. There is .... milk in the fridge.
10. She can't eat .... salad.
11. We spent .... money during the last summer vacation.
12. We didn't spend .... money during the last summer vacation.
13. They couldn't take .... pictures when they were on vacation.
14. I won't be able to meet you. I have .... work to do tomorrow.
15. She doesn't put .... salt in her food.

(A) LITTLE / (A) FEW

- (A) *little* is used with an uncountable noun.
  (a) little water, (a) little soup, (a) little time
- (A) few is used with a plural noun.
  (a) few books, (a) few people, (a) few days

A little / a few is a positive idea.

(28) There is *a little water* in the tank. (some water)
(29) *A few people* attended the meeting. (some people)

Little / few without (a) before them is a negative idea.

(30) There is *little water* in the tank. (not much)
(31) *Few people* attended the meeting. (not many)

EXERCISE 5 (ADVANCED)

Fill in the blanks with *little, few, a little, a few.*

1. You can apply for a job in this company. There are still .... jobs lying vacant.
2. I didn't eat anything last night. There was ...... food left on the table.
3. He can't buy this car as he has .... money left.
4. Let's hurry up! We've .... time to catch the train.
5. Let's have some more coke. There's .... coke left in the bottle.
6. We don't watch TV any more, as there are .... good programmes shown these days.

7. I need .... water to dilute this colour.
8. We enjoyed the party last evening. .... of my old friends came to attend the party.
9. He is not a well-known writer. .... people have heard of him.
10. There are still .... good teachers in this college.
11. I didn't like the food as there was .... salt put in it.
12. We've .... good players in our team; so we're going to win this match.
13. We've .... good players in our team; so we're going to lose this match.
14. I needn't write any letters today. I've already written .... letters today.
15. There is .... water in the bottle; so you may buy a bottle of mineral water.

Unit 9

MAIN VERBS

REGULAR VERBS

A main verb usually has five forms:

Base form	-s / -es	Past tense	Past participle	Present participle
present tense	with the third person singular subject in the present tense			
work start go	works starts started goes went	worked started went	worked started gone	working starting going

EXERCISE 1 (ELEMENTARY)

Underline the main verbs in the following sentences.

1. The bird flies in the sky.
2. Edward talks loudly.
3. Mr Johnson and Ms Antony teach us English.
4. The door opened.
5. They work in our school.
6. The cat and the dog ran after the rat.
7. We danced all night.
8. I wrote a letter in the morning.
9. The donkey carries weight.
10. They sang at the party.
11. We eat dinner at 8 o'clock in the evening.
12. She gave me a flower.

13. The lion roared loudly.
14. My father likes tea.
15. The children play in the evening.

Rules for the use of the different forms of verbs

- We use the base form of the verb in the present tense with the following nouns/pronouns:
  I, we, you, they, and plural nouns like *boys, girls, Rakesh and Lata, John and Mary* etc.
  (1) I *go* to school at eight in the morning.
  (2) They *work* in a company.
  (3) Rakesh and Lata *watch* TV in the morning.
- We use *-s* or *-es* with the base form of the verb in the present tense with the following nouns/pronouns:
  He, she, it and singular forms of nouns *boy, girl, Rakesh, Mira, Edward, Jane* etc.
  (4) He *goes* to school at eight in the morning.
  (5) This girl *plays* tennis in the evening.
  (6) Mira *drives* her car fast.
- We use the past form of the verb in the past tense with any noun/pronoun. Usually, we may use a word like *yesterday, last week, last month, in 1987* etc. with the past form of the verb.
  (7) Abishek gave me his book yesterday.
  (8) My parents *visited* us last month.
- We use the present participle (-ing) form of the main verb with *is, am, are, was* and *were.*
  (9) I *am reading* this book these days.
  (10) They *are watching* the news.
  (11) He *was playing* football yesterday in the evening.
- We use the past participle (-ed) form of the verb with *has, have* or *had*. We may use words such as *just, recently, already* etc.
  (12) She *has finished* her work just now.
  (13) They *have already eaten* lunch.

Exercise 2 (elementary)

Fill in the blanks with the correct form of the verb given within brackets.

1. She has already .... this medicine. (test)
2. I .... till 2 o'clock yesterday. (work)
3. She is .... at him. (laugh)
4. They have just .... their work. (complete)
5. Mukesh was .... with Rekha at the party. (dance)
6. My mother .... fish for us yesterday. (fry)
7. Radha and Shyam are .... as they are sick. (cough)
8. We .... ten miles last Sunday. (walk)
9. I am .... a letter. (write)
10. They are .... to finish the work. (try)
11. She .... in the bathroom yesterday. (slip)
12. We have already .... the money. (receive)
13. Mukesh .... in this building. (live)
14. John and Bill .... a tiger yesterday. (kill)
15. She has just .... our house.(reach)
16. I .... my father very much. (love)
17. She .... the class 10 examination last year. (pass)
18. The train has .... near the bridge. (stop)
19. We always .... special spices to make this dish. (use)
20. He is in trouble. He .... your help. (need)

Irregular Main Verbs

Irregular verbs are like regular verbs in their *-s* or *-es* forms and in their *-ing* (present participle forms.) However, their past and past participle forms do not take *-d* or *-ed*.

Base	Past	Past Participle
write	wrote	written
break	broke	broken
go	went	gone

A few verbs have a common form for the base, past and past participle forms:

Base	Past	Past Participle
cut	cut	cut
hit	hit	hit

Exercise 3 (intermediate)

Fill in the blanks with the correct form of the verbs given within brackets.

1. She .... a letter yesterday (write).
2. My father has .... his term (complete).
3. I .... this job (like).
4. Mary is .... a novel (read).
5. John .... to office by car (go).
6. They are .... the wood in the room (cut).
7. Umesh always .... his car fast (drive).
8. I have .... Mukesh for five years (know).
9. They have .... the construction of their house (start).
10. They are .... in the hall (dance).
11. Yuvraj has .... a century (hit).
12. The match .... at 10 o'clock yesterday (begin).
13. The sun .... in the east (rise).
14. They are .... coke in the lawn (drink).
15. This book .... rupees thirty (cost).
16. The bell is .... (ring).
17. Our dog .... last month (die).
18. We .... Lucknow in 1992 (leave).
19. She .... in the afternoon (sleep).
20. They have .... the window (break).
21. She .... me a present yesterday (give).
22. I have already .... the bill (pay).
23. Monica .... a song at the party (sing).
24. He has just .... the bell (ring).
25. The examination .... on time on Monday (begin).
26. She is .... in the corner near the door (sit).
27. He .... the ball with his hand during yesterday's match (stop).
28. She has just .... out to meet her friend (go).
29. I have already .... this book (read).
30. My brother .... in the afternoon (sleep).

Unit 10

AUXILIARY VERBS

In Unit 9 we discussed the different forms of the main verb. There can be other verbs occurring with the main verbs and are called *auxiliaries* or *helping verbs.* In some cases there can be one, two or more auxiliaries used in front of the main verb.

(1) Razia *is* sleeping inside.
(2) Veena *has* finished her work.
(3) Mukesh and Lina *were* watching TV last evening.
(4) They *did* not meet us yesterday.
(5) I *will* write to him tomorrow.
(6) They *have been* living in Lucknow for five years.

Notice that *is, has, were, did, will* and *have been* are auxiliaries or helping verbs and *sleeping, finished, watching, meet, write* and *living* are main verbs in the sentences above.

EXERCISE 1 (ELEMENTARY)

Underline the auxiliaries and main verbs in the following sentences. Label them as VA and VM.

1. Mary has been watching TV in her room since morning.
2. They have read this novel.
3. When I went to see them, they were playing cricket.
4. Sarada had written to me earlier also.
5. They will be meeting us in Delhi next month.
6. He does not like this food.
7. Sakshi has closed the door.
8. We will attend her class tomorrow.
9. My father is taking a bath.
10. The train had already left when I reached the station.
11. Joan will travel to Kanpur tomorrow.
12. She has already watched this film.
13. I do not know anyone in this town.
14. She did not meet us at the airport.
15. I am visiting her next week.

EXERCISE 2 (ELEMENTARY)

Fill in the blanks with the auxiliaries given below.

is, am, are, was, were, has, have, had, will or shall.

1. She .... singing in the hall. Can you hear?
2. I .... sleeping, when she phoned me yesterday.
3. I .... meet him tomorrow.
4. She .... already watched this film.
5. We .... working, when our officer visited us yesterday.
6. She .... already finished the lecture, when we reached college.
7. The children .... playing in the park. You can see them from here.
8. Vaibhav and Rekha .... driving the car.
9. They .... purchased a new house recently.
10. When I went to see them, they .... playing cricket.
11. My brother .... opened a new shop.
12. I .... writing a novel these days.
13. The plane .... left, before we reached the airport.
14. My mother .... cooking dinner.
15. We .... go to Mumbai next week.
16. Our cook .... already washed the dishes.
17. They .... finished their work.
18. Mira .... reach the US tomorrow.
19. I .... meet you in ten minutes. I .... writing a letter now.
20. They .... just left for Delhi.

Unit 11

'BE' AND 'HAVE' AND MODAL AUXILIARIES

'BE' AS A MAIN VERB

The verb 'be' can be used as a main verb. The other forms of 'be' – *is, am, are, was* and *were* – can also be used as main verbs. We usually use a noun or an adjective and sometimes, an adverbial, after the verb 'be'. As a main verb, 'be' is a linking verb.

(1) Her mother *is* a doctor.
(2) I *am* hungry.
(3) Rajinder *was* very quick.

EXERCISE 1 (INTERMEDIATE)

Fill in the blanks with *is, am, are, was* or *were*.

1. She .... twenty years old today.
   She .... nineteen last year.
2. Mukesh .... an army officer.
3. Rita and Madhavi .... very tired.
4. My brother .... in the library and my sister .... in the lecture hall.
5. I .... very tired. I walked five miles today.
6. The BA I students .... downstairs and the BA II students .... in the canteen.
7. Her brother .... pilot.
8. He .... a very tall person but his late father .... not so.
9. They .... very healthy in their childhood but now they .... not.
10. Today .... Tuesday; yesterday .... Monday.

'HAVE' AS A MAIN VERB

Have, has and *had* can be used as main verbs to express possession. We can also use *have got, has got* and *had got* to express possession.

(4) I *have/have got* three dogs. (I possess/own three dogs).
(5) She *has/has got* a new cycle.

We may also use *have/has got* to mean *have/has obtained* or *have/has received*.

(6) I *have* just *got* a letter from Mukta.

Exercise 2 (intermediate)

Replace the underlined words with *have, has, had, have got, has got* or *had got*. In some cases it is possible to use both *have/has/had* and *have/has/had got*.

1. She owns a factory near my house.
2. They possess a brand new car.
3. I own a beautiful dress.
4. She said that she owned a car when she was young.
5. Sarika and her husband own a house in Chandigarh.
6. I have just received a letter from my uncle.
7. When I saw her, she had just bought a new car.
8. I had just obtained the loan from the bank, when I received my appointment letter.
9. They own a spare scooter.
10. She possesses five books on Shakespeare.

'Have' can also be used to refer to a number of actions such as *eating, drinking, enjoying,* etc.

(7) We *had* lunch at 2 o'clock yesterday.
(8) She *has* a good sense of humour.
(9) They *had* a wonderful party.

Exercise 3 (advanced)

Make sentences with *have* + the words in brackets.

1. (a wonderful vacation): *I had a wonderful vacation last month.*
2. (a good lunch)
3. (sugar in tea)
4. (a headache)
5. (a haircut)
6. (a pain in the ankle)
7. (a lovely evening)
8. (a wonderful day)
9. (a bad cold)
10. (breakfast)

Modal Auxiliaries

There are ten *modals* or *modal auxiliaries* in English: *can, could, may, might, will, would, shall, should, must* and *ought to.* Each one of these modal auxiliaries has a special meaning. We shall learn about their meanings in Units 31, 32 and 33. Modal auxiliaries are used before main verbs or before other auxiliaries.

(10) She *can* lift eighty kilos.
(11) Mukesh *might* have done it.

Exercise 4 (elementary)

Underline the modal auxiliaries, auxiliaries and main verbs in the following sentences. Label them as MA, VA and VM.

1. Joan will be taking our class tomorrow.
2. Meena could have written a letter to you.
3. She has been reading this book since morning.
4. You ought to respect your parents.
5. I shall visit your office tomorrow.
6. You may take leave on Tuesday.
7. Madhuri might be in the library.
8. We should finish the work this evening.
9. She may be sleeping inside.
10. I must go to the airport now.
11. She was having her lunch, when I visited her yesterday.
12. It will rain tomorrow.
13. I can see a car outside.
14. They had already left when I reached their home yesterday.
15. They should have received you at the airport.
16. When I met him last, he looked rather young.
17. My father goes to office by car.
18. Her mother is a university professor.
19. My brother might come here in the evening.
20. She has already given me money.

Unit 12

THE SIMPLE PRESENT AND PRESENT CONTINUOUS TENSES

THE SIMPLE PRESENT TENSE

Form

In order to write a sentence in the simple present tense, we use the first form of the verb. However, if the subject is in the third person singular (*he, she, it, Nilima, Sohrab,* etc.) we use the first form of the verb followed by the suffixes *-s* or *-es.*

If the subject is the first person singular or plural (*I* or *we*), second person singular or plural (*you* or *you*), or the third person plural (*they, Nilima, Sohrab* etc.) we use only the first form of the verb.

Add *-s* to most of the verbs, if the subject is a third person singular noun or pronoun.

give / gives, play / plays, laugh / laughs

Add *-es* to the verbs ending in

-o,	go/goes
-s,	miss/misses
-x,	mix/mixes
-ch/-sh,	catch/catches
	lash/lashes

(1) She *sleeps* till eight o'clock in the morning.
(2) He *goes* to office by bus.
(3) They *work* in a bank.
(4) I *write* to my wife every week.

EXERCISE 1 (INTERMEDIATE)

Change the subject underlined to the third person singular and add *-s* or *-es* to the verb. Make necessary changes wherever required.

1. They go to college by bus. *He goes* to college by bus.
2. They want to visit Amritsar next week as their sons have to take the medical entrance test.

3. They drink a lot of milk in the morning and then they exercise in the garden.
4. They often forget things.
5. My sisters love eating fish.
6. My friends drive slowly.
7. They always wash their hands before meals.
8. Dogs enjoy eating meat.
9. Horses always eat grass.
10. They go to office by train but come back home by bus.
11. They pay Rs 3000 per month as rent for their house.
12. My brothers have mobile phones and often ring me up in the evening.
13. The boys in our room get up at seven in the morning and have breakfast by eight.
14. These men work in my office.
15. My friends leave for Mumbai next week. They always spend their vacation in another city.
16. They always wear new clothes on New Year's Day.
17. Babies always cry a lot.
18. Their children hate drinking milk but love eating chocolates.
19. These girls often pass your house.
20. These men wear very colourful clothes.

EXERCISE 2 (INTERMEDIATE)

Rewrite the following sentences, using the noun/noun phrase given in brackets. Make the necessary changes in the verb.

1. He runs very fast. (they)
   They run very fast.
2. I go for a long walk in the evening. (we)
   We go for a long walk in the evening.
3. She walks to college every morning and looks for her friends on the way. (they)
4. That boy plays cricket very well. (those boys) He plays cricket every evening. (they)
5. I often watch a film on TV in the evening. (we)
6. You manage your accounts so well. (they)
7. This chair costs Rs 300. (these chairs)
8. He has his lunch at 1 pm. (they)
9. She goes to work by bus and comes home on foot. (they)
10. That girl wants to talk to you. (those girls)

11. I sometimes go to sleep at midnight. (they)
12. You know English well. (we)
13. A baby needs a lot of attention. (babies) It needs milk four to five times in a day. (they)
14. A lion roars loudly. (lions)
15. I drink a lot of milk in the evening. (we)

Uses of the simple present tense

- *Habitual actions:* This use is achieved through the use of adverbials such as *always, often, generally, usually, everyday, every week* etc. along with the verb in simple present tense.
  (5) We *visit* Shimla every year.
  (6) My father *goes* to work by car.
- *General or permanent truths:*
  (7) The earth *revolves* around the sun.
  (8) Honesty *is* the best policy.
- *Thoughts and feelings at the present moment:*
  (9) She *is* tired.
  (10) Maria *looks* weak.
- *Commentaries and demonstrations:*
  (11) Kapil Dev *bowls* to Imran Khan. Imran Khan *hits* the ball and Sidhu *stops* the ball at mid-on.
  (12) *Take* four eggs and a pinch of salt. *Beat* the eggs in a bowl and then add salt.
- *Future*: for events related to time tables and programmes, or something which is the result of a 'natural law':
  (13) The train *leaves* at 6.30 pm.
  (14) The sun *rises* at 5.30 am tomorrow.

EXERCISE 3 (ELEMENTARY)

Write the following sentences choosing the correct form of the verbs in the brackets.

1. The matinee show (begin) at 3.30 pm and (end) at 6.00 pm.
2. We (leave) for Udaipur tomorrow.
3. The sun (rise) in the east.
4. He (look) tall in the black suit.
5. Water (boil) at 100°C.
6. I (go) to University on cycle.

7. We (play) hockey in the evening.
8. (Pour) milk and cream in the bowl and (whisk) them.
9. Dickens (describe) the social life of the nineteenth century in his novels.
10. This peak (remain) snow-clad throughout the year.
11. Rajesh and Meera (wear) glasses.
12. She (drive) to her school every morning.
13. Iron (turn) red when heated.
14. They (reach) their office at 9 o'clock in the morning.
15. She (write) to her father every week.
16. Rakesh (pass) the ball to Balbir and Balbir (send) it across to Vijay.
17. The bus (leave) at 8 o'clock this evening.
18. The play (start) at 6 o'clock next Monday.
19. She (look) very charming in the white dress.
20. Summers (be) very hot in India.
21. We usually (take) dinner at 8 o'clock in the evening.
22. The sun (set) in the West.
23. It (rain) here practically everyday in summer.
24. Colonel Naik (walk) towards the President. He (salute) the President.
25. Sita and Rajni (play) the veena every evening.

The Present Continuous Tense

Form

The present continuous is formed with the present form of the auxiliary *be* (*is/am/are*) + the *present participle* (V+ing) form of the main verb.

(15) Reema *is reading* a book.
(16) *I am writing* a letter.

If a verb ends in *-e*, we omit the *-e* and add *-ing*. For example, *use/using.*

(17) She *is using* my calculator.

If a verb has a single vowel followed by a single consonant, we double the final consonant: *hit/hitting.*

(18) He *is hitting* the bat on the ground.

If a verb is a two-syllable word and the second syllable is stressed, we double the last consonant: *be'gin/be'ginning.*

(19) The car *is beginning* to start.

We change *-ie* to *-y*: *lie/lying*.

(20) She *is lying* on the bed.

EXERCISE 4 (ELEMENTARY)

Fill in the blanks with the present continuous tense of the verbs given in brackets.

1. She .... her new dress. (put on)
2. I .... a letter. (write)
3. I .... of hunger. (die)
4. They .... by car. (travel)
5. He .... the play on TV. (watch)
6. We .... the luggage. (carry)
7. She .... for you outside. (wait)
8. They .... in the ground. (run)
9. He .... tea in a glass. (drink)
10. We .... under the tree. (lie)
11. I .... rice. (eat)
12. She .... in a chair. (sit)
13. She .... a horse. (ride)
14. He .... outside. (weep)
15. She .... in the pool outside. (swim)
16. Padma .... a beautiful song. (sing)
17. They .... now. (sleep)
18. She .... utensils. (clean)
19. They .... the bus. (stop)
20. She .... (cry)

Uses of the present continuous tense

The present continuous tense is used:

- for actions that are happening or are in progress at the present moment. We may use adverbials such as *now, in the morning, just,* etc.

  (21) Ted is sleeping in the room. (at the present moment)
  (22) She is just having her lunch.

- to describe temporary situations, happenings which are not habitual actions but are thought to be happening for a limited period.

(23a) I'm working in a bank these days. (I don't usually work in a bank)

(23b) I work in a bank. (habitual situation)

- to express future with reference to a definite *plan*, *arrangement* or *programme*. Usually, an adverbial of future time such as *tomorrow*, *tonight*, *next week*, *on Monday* etc. is used.

(24) We're leaving for Ahmedabad tomorrow.

(25) The train is leaving at 8 o'clock tonight.

- to express repeated action referring to habitual actions. Adverbials such as *always*, *continually*, *constantly*, *repeatedly*, etc. are used to describe repeated actions.

(26) She is always talking about her achievements.

(27) He is repeatedly asking for money.

Exercise 5 (elementary)

Fill in the blanks with the present continuous tense of the verbs in brackets.

1. She .... tennis there. (play)
2. The DD Metro .... 'Gandhi' tomorrow. (show)
3. Vijay .... in the library. (study)
4. Sudha .... as an accountant in our firm for a month. (work)
5. He .... the door. (close)
6. Shalini .... for you in her office. (wait)
7. She .... a sweater for her husband. (knit)
8. It .... outside. (rain)
9. Vanita .... to her sister. (talk)
10. They .... noise in class. (always, make)
11. The carpenter .... my table at the moment. (repair)
12. She .... in her house. (constantly sing)
13. She generally plays badminton but she .... cricket today. (play)
14. I .... my doctor tonight. (visit)
15. She .... to herself. (always hum)

Exercise 6 (intermediate)

Fill in the blanks with the present continuous or simple present tense of the verbs in brackets.

1. In India, women usually .... saris. (wear)
2. The train .... at the station. (arrive)

3. They .... with their parents till they get official accommodation. (stay)
4. She usually .... yoga in the morning but nowadays she .... it in the evening. (practise, practise)
5. The plane .... at 5 o'clock tomorrow. (leave)
6. Our college .... at 9 o'clock everyday. (start)
7. Monica generally .... for a walk in the evening, but this evening she .... (go, rest)
8. John .... very hard. (work). These days he .... for an entrance examination. (prepare)
9. They .... your plan in the office of the General Manager. (just discuss)
10. We .... for Chennai on Monday. (leave)
11. She .... in the class. (always speak)
12. Meeta .... with her left hand but she .... to write with her right hand. (write, try)
13. Shailaja .... in honour of the Chief Guest. (sing)
14. She .... her lecture now. (give)
15. She .... her lecture in the morning. (give)
16. I .... cooking food but today my husband .... the dinner. (enjoy, cook)
17. I .... a man outside. He .... to say something. (see, try)
18. Someone .... at the door (knock). Could you go and see who it is?
19. He .... an umbrella but today he .... a raincoat. (always carry, carry)
20. I .... to lock the door. (always forget)

Stative and dynamic verbs

Stative verbs refer to a state, quality, or condition. Stative verbs are usually not used in the continuous (*-ing*) form.

(28) I see a man outside (*not* I'm seeing…)
(29) I forget his name. (*not* I'm forgetting…)

Stative verbs can be divided into three broad categories.

- *Relational verbs*: be, have, contain, belong, matter, consist, own.
- *Perception verbs*: see, hear, feel, smell, taste, etc.
- *Attitudinal verbs*: assume, believe, dislike, expect, feel, forget, hate, hope, know, like, love, mind, notice, remember, see, think, understand, want, wish, etc.

Dynamic verbs can be used either in their simple or in their continuous forms.

(30a) She plays in the field. (simple present tense)
(30b) She is playing in the field. (present continuous)
(31a) She reads novels. (simple present tense)
(31b) She is reading novels. (present continuous)

Dynamic verbs can be divided into four broad categories:

- *Action verbs*: write, read, ask, work, play, walk, run, call, laugh etc.
- *Intransitive verbs*: arrive, change, die, draw, stop, etc.
- *Some sensation and linking verbs*: burn, feel, glow, hurt, get, become, grow, and turn
- *Momentary verbs*: shake, knock, nod, jump, open, close, hit, shoot, tap, etc.

EXERCISE 7 (ADVANCED)

Fill in the blanks with an appropriate tense of the verbs given in brackets. For a dynamic verb, use the present continuous tense and for a stative verb, use the simple present tense.

1. She .... at the door. (knock)
2. Roger .... after the dogs. (run)
3. This box .... salt. (contain)
4. I .... this house. (own)
5. Aziz .... a book in the room. (read)
6. The peon .... the door. (open)
7. All the patients .... (improve)
8. The train .... over the bridge. (stop)
9. I .... her. (dislike)
10. Shailaja .... brown eyes. (have)
11. I .... something burning. (smell)
12. He .... his head. (shake)
13. They .... loudly at her. (laugh)
14. The flower .... its colour. (change)
15. Our house .... to my grandfather. (belong)
16. This food .... good. (taste)
17. She .... her head. (nod)
18. They .... for ten hours these days. (work)
19. They .... after the cat. (run)
20. She .... tall. (grow)

Unit 13

THE SIMPLE PAST AND THE PRESENT PERFECT TENSES

The Simple Past

Form

- Regular verbs end with *-d* or *-ed* in the simple past.
  - (1) We *watched* TV last evening.
  - (2) She *lied* to me.
- But the simple past of irregular verbs is not formed by the addition of *-d* or *-ed*. Some have the root form functioning as the past and past participle form.

  hit – hit – hit

  put – put – put

  - (3) He *hit* a century.
- Some irregular verbs have the *past* and *past participle* forms different from the root form, but both the forms are the same.

  tell – told – told

  keep – kept – kept

  - (4) My aunt *told* us a story every evening.
- Some irregular verbs have different *past* and *past participle* forms.

  know – knew – known

  break – broke – broken

  - (5) She *broke* the cup in the morning.

Exercise 1 (elementary)

Fill in the blanks with the past forms of the verbs underlined in the first sentence.

1. I visit Goa every year.
   I visited Goa last year also.
2. She sings beautifully. She .... at the party last night.
3. We play hockey every Sunday. We .... hockey last Sunday.

4. He locks the door every morning. He .... the door yesterday.
5. We always meet on Friday. We .... last Friday.
6. Sachin usually makes a century. Sachin .... a century in the last test match.
7. She always puts on a white dress. Yesterday, she .... a blue dress.
8. They usually sleep in the train. Last Monday, they .... in the train.
9. She cleans the house every evening. But yesterday, she .... the house in the morning.
10. I write letters every day. Yesterday, I .... five letters.
11. She stops her car in the middle of the road. She .... her car on the side of the road yesterday.
12. I don't like dogs now but I .... dogs when I was young.
13. They sell old furniture. They .... old cars ten years ago.
14. I often see Sarika. I .... her yesterday.
15. He obeys the officer's orders. He .... the officer's orders, when he was new.
16. She cuts vegetables before cooking. She .... vegetables before cooking in the morning.
17. He knows her well. He .... her well, when they were children.
18. Where did you buy this book? I .... it from the Universal Book Depot.
19. How did you travel? I .... by car.
20. How did it break? It .... while we were lifting it.

Uses of the simple past tense

The simple past tense is used for events, actions or situations which happened in the past and are complete. The action/event could have happened in the recent or distant past. We usually use adverbials of time with the simple past: *yesterday, last week, last month, last year, on Friday, at 2 pm., in 1994* etc. Sometimes it is used with an adverbial of time and the word *ago*: *two days ago, a minute ago* etc.

The simple past can even be used with an adverbial clause of time introduced by conjunctions such as *when, while, till, before* and *after.*

(6) We *translated* ten pages *yesterday.*

(7) I *met* Rita *at the airport.*
(8) I *saw* her *a minute ago.*
(9) I *waited* for you *till the lecture was over.*

Exercise 2 (intermediate)

Write the complete answers to the following questions using the adverbials in brackets.

1. When did you last see 'Sholay'? (I was in class 10)
   I last saw 'Sholay' when I was in class 10.
2. When did Shefali join your college? (a fortnight ago)
3. Where did Rahul go last night? (to the hostel)
4. How long did you wait at the station? (till they arrived)
5. When did his wife cook dinner? (while he was watching TV)
6. When did you begin to learn French? (when I was in class 8)
7. When did Jane attend the meeting? (on Monday)
8. When did you join this company? (a month ago)
9. Where did they spend their vacation last year? (in Shimla)
10. How did you travel to Ooty? (by car)
11. Where did you meet her? (at the station)
12. When did she sell her car? (last month)
13. How did she eat apples? (slowly)
14. When did he drink milk? (in the morning)
15. When did your father buy this house? (last year)
16. Where did she lose her watch? (at the party)
17. Where did she keep the milk? (in the fridge)
18. Where did she put the keys? (on the table)
19. When did you write this essay? (a week ago)
20. How did it break? (I was keeping it on the shelf)

The Present Perfect Tense

Form

The present perfect tense is formed by using the auxiliary verb *have* and the past participle form of the main verb.

(10) I *have* recently *seen* this film.

We use *has* with the third person singular subject *he, she, it, Rakesh* etc.

(11) She *has started* a new shop.

The past participle often ends in *-d* or *-ed* (*started, opened*) but many important verbs are irregular (*spoken, written, done, put,* etc.).

Uses of the present perfect tense

- We use the present perfect tense to express an action which began in the past and continues up to the present.

  (12) I've worked in this college for five years.

- We can use this tense to express something that happened only a short time ago. We usually use the adverbs *just, recently,* and *already* to express this meaning.

  (13) Mukta has already finished her dinner.

- We may also use this tense for actions which happened at an unspecified time in the past.

  (14) I've been a taxi driver. (sometime in the past)
  (15) I've seen this film.

- We often use the present perfect to give new information.

  (16) Malcolm X has just been assassinated.

Exercise 3 (elementary)

Fill in the blanks with the present perfect tense of the verbs in brackets.

1. I .... this film. (already see)
2. They .... a new car. (recently buy)
3. The Prime Minister .... (resign)
4. Renuka .... in this bank for seven years. (work)
5. I .... this novel. (write)
6. She .... to me. (already speak)
7. They .... to the exhibition. (be)
8. We .... this film. (recently see)
9. She .... your letters. (post)
10. She .... with an accident. (met)
11. I .... six pages so far. (type)
12. They .... this problem for five days. (work on)
13. He .... in this hostel since 1998. (live)
14. I .... the blackboard. (just clean)
15. Varoon .... joined the IIT. (just join)
16. Rakesh .... this car for seven years. (drive)

17. I .... him for ten years. (know)
18. He .... your application to the District Magistrate. (send)
19. Veronica .... a college lecturer. (recently become)
20. Rita .... these clothes. (just wash)

The simple past and the present perfect

We use the simple past when we want to specify when something happened.

(17) I *finished* this work *yesterday/two hours ago.*

We use the present perfect when we do not want to specify *when* something happened. We use only adverbials such as *recently, just,* etc., which do not specify time.

(18) I've (just) finished this work.

We usually use the present perfect with *today, this morning, this evening, this month* etc., though it is possible to use the simple past with these adverbials.

EXERCISE 4 (ADVANCED)

Fill in the blanks using the simple past or the present perfect forms of the verbs given in brackets.

1. I .... a car in my life. (never drive)
2. I .... her since she left Lucknow. (not see)
3. They .... this house last year. (buy)
4. We .... to them for a week now. (not write)
5. She .... a doctor in July, and now they .... to live in Mumbai. (marry, go)
6. She .... a doctor in July, and then they .... to live in Mumbai. (marry, go)
7. My younger brother .... this job last month. (get)
8. My younger brother .... this job. (recently got)
9. I .... my dinner an hour ago. (have)
10. I .... my dinner. (just have)
11. Many teachers .... this University since 1995. (join)
12. My sister .... to Chennai in 1991 but I .... there even once. (go, not, have)
13. I .... such a man in my life. (never see)
14. I .... the store yesterday. (clean)
15. I .... the store. (recently clean)

16. The doctor .... me a few tablets when he came to our house, but I .... them yet. (give, not take)
17. I .... to my sister for two months. (not write)
18. My sister .... this office two months ago. (leave)
19. They .... Delhi a month ago. (visit)
20. They .... Delhi. (recently visit)

Unit 14

THE PRESENT PERFECT CONTINUOUS TENSE

Form

The present perfect continuous tense is formed by *has been/have been + the present participle (v +ing)* form of the main verb. *Has been* is used in the case of third person singular subjects.

(1) Rita *has been working* with us since 1997.

(2) *I've been painting* this room since morning.

Uses of the present perfect continuous tense

- The present perfect continuous may be used to refer to an action that started in the past and is still happening.
  - (3) We've been living in this house since childhood.
  - (4) She has been watching television for two hours.
- It may also refer to an action that ended in the recent past.
  - (5) I've been trying to solve this problem. (but now I've stopped)
  - (6) It has been raining. (but it stopped a short while ago)
- The present perfect continuous may also refer to the result of a past action.
  - (7) Your eyes are red. You've been crying.
  - (8) Your house is leaking. Has the overhead tank been overflowing?

Exercise 1 (elementary)

Fill in the blanks with the present perfect continuous tense of the verbs in brackets.

1. I .... in this office for ten years. (work)
2. She .... under the tree for two hours. (stand)
3. Pranay .... your car. (repair)
4. They .... the meat since morning. (cook)
5. We .... here since 1984. (live)
6. He .... the whole day and now he is tired. (play)
7. The dog .... all through the night. (bark)
8. My sisters .... this school since 1978. (run)

9. They .... since morning. (practise)
10. It .... for the last ten days. (rain)
11. Vikas .... for the last four hours. (study)
12. She .... since evening. (sing)
13. I .... this car for two years. (drive)
14. I .... in this school since 1990. (teach)
15. They .... outside for a long time. (sit)

EXERCISE 2 (ADVANCED)

Read the following sentences. Use the words given in brackets and write a sentence in the present perfect continuous tense.

1. Vandana looks very tired. (she/work/hard/all day)
   She has been working hard all day.
2. His eyes are red. (He/cry)
3. They are thirsty. (They/play/cricket/the whole day)
4. She is sleeping now. (She/watch/TV/all day)
5. The ground is wet. (It/rain)
6. He is standing outside. (He/wait/for you/since morning)
7. They are sitting in the drawing room. (They/discuss/your plan/for two hours)
8. She is out of breath. (She/run)
9. They are tired. (They/drive/all through the day)
10. He is very hungry. (He/travel/since yesterday)

EXERCISE 3 (ADVANCED)

Read the following pairs of sentences. With the help of each pair write a sentence saying how long something has been happening.

1. I'm living in this house. I started living here in 1980.
   I've been living in this house since 1980.
2. The baby is crying. The baby started crying an hour ago.
   .... for an hour.
3. She works in the post office. She started working in the post office in 1995.
   .... since 1995.
4. He is reading a novel. He started reading the novel last week.
   .... since last week.
5. They're learning French. They started learning French five years ago.
   .... for five years.
6. Ahmed is studying. He began studying two hours ago.

.... for two hours.

7. Rohan plays cricket. He began playing cricket in 1996.
   .... since 1996.
8. Mukesh flies planes. He started flying planes in 1990.
   .... since 1990.
9. It is raining now. It began raining on Tuesday.
   .... since Tuesday.
10. I'm swimming now. I started swimming an hour ago.
   .... for an hour.

The present perfect and the present perfect continuous

- We use the present perfect continuous to indicate that the action is unfinished and, therefore, continues.

  (9) She has been reading this book since Monday. (and she is still reading it).

- We use the present perfect to indicate that the action is finished/ complete.

  (10) She has read this book/three books.

- We use the present perfect continuous to say how long something has been happening.

  (11) He has been playing hockey for three hours.

- We use the present perfect to say how much we have done/how many things we have done/how many times we have done something.

  (12) He has played hockey three times today.

- With some verbs such as *know* and *understand* we only use the present perfect tense.

  (13) I've known him for a long time.

EXERCISE 4 (ADVANCED)

Construct sentences in present perfect/present perfect continuous tense using the words/phrases given in the brackets. Remember to begin with a capital letter and end with a full stop.

1. (Mary/teach/Shakespeare/for four months)
   Mary has been teaching Shakespeare for four months.
2. (Mary/teach/two plays/until now)
   Mary has taught two plays until now.
3. Parvez/study/political science/three months.

4. Parvez/study/four chapters/so far.
5. Manoj/travelling/around India/for six months.
6. He/visit/four states/so far.
7. My brothers/sell/TV sets/since they left college.
8. My brothers/sell/more than a thousand TV sets/since they left college.
9. They/count/money/since morning.
10. They/counted/fifty bundles/until now.

Use of *for* and *since*: *For* and *since* are generally used with the present perfect or the present perfect continuous tense.

- *For* is used to express a *period* of time.

  for ten minutes, for eight years, for a long time.

  (14) We've lived in this house for twenty years.

  (15) He has been using your telephone for the last two years.

- *Since* is used to express a *point* of time.

  since morning, since Friday, since 1991, since last week, since 10 o'clock

Exercise 5 (intermediate)

Fill in the blanks with *for* or *since*.

1. It has been raining .... yesterday.
2. They've been playing football .... the last two hours.
3. My father has been ill .... Sunday.
4. I have taught in this college .... four years.
5. She has been cooking .... evening.
6. Radhika has been living in this flat .... the last ten years.
7. Radhika has been living in this flat .... 1991.
8. They've been fighting for the voting right .... three years.
9. We've not bought any clothes .... the beginning of this year.
10. My daughter has studied in this school .... ten years.
11. I've been a doctor .... five years.
12. She has been an invalid .... her childhood.
13. The dog has been barking .... morning.
14. They've been watching TV .... the last three hours.
15. I've been driving .... 1999.
16. Our teacher has been on leave .... two days.
17. Our Principal has been teaching us .... our English teacher went on leave.
18. We've been studying German .... six months.
19. We've been studying German .... January.
20. My daughter has used this bag .... three years.

Unit 15

THE PAST CONTINUOUS TENSE

Form

The past continuous tense is formed by using *was/were* + the present participle (*-ing*) form of the main verb.

(1) They *were sleeping* when I visited them.

Uses of the past continuous tense

- The past continuous is used for actions which were in progress or continued in the past. It does not indicate the beginning or the end of the action. It may be used with a specific point of time.

  (2) They were playing football at 5 pm yesterday.(they were playing before 5 pm also)

  (3) She was waiting for her car at 11 am yesterday.

- The past continuous is more often used in a complex sentence. The main clause may be in the past continuous tense and the adverbial clause of time with the conjunction *when* may be in the simple past tense.

  (4) When the bell rang, she was studying in the library.

  (5) Rakesh *was sharpening* a pencil, when the lights went out.

- It is possible to use the adverbial clause beginning with *while*, or *just as* in the past continuous, describing an action or event.

  (6) While I was entering the lift, the door closed.

  (7) Just as we were leaving office, it began to rain.

- The past continuous is also used with adverbials beginning with *all*: *all right*, *all evening* etc. Notice that the adverbials express continuity.

  (8) Mallaya was talking all evening yesterday.

  (9) It was raining all last week.

Exercise 1 (elementary)

Rewrite the following sentences. Use the past continuous form of the verb in brackets.

1. She (leave) school when I saw her.
2. While I (cross) the road, she waved at me.
3. I entered the room while she (teaching) her class.
4. She (drive) her car when she saw the accident.
5. We (played) football all evening yesterday.
6. I (listen to) the evening news when I heard a knock at the door.
7. They (play) cricket in the morning yesterday.
8. We (watching) TV at 7.30 in the evening yesterday.
9. They (sit) in the library when the Principal called them to his office.
10. She (have) her lunch when I went to meet her.
11. Monica jumped off the train while it (move).
12. They burst crackers while we (study).
13. We (walk) home when it started raining.
14. He (teach) all through the day on Monday.
15. He (play) the piano all evening.
16. Bina (type) a letter when Dr Singh called her.
17. She cooked dinner while her husband (write) letters.
18. My mother (make) cake when the lights went out.
19. They (sleep) all evening yesterday.
20. The phone rang while I (taking) a bath.

Exercise 2 (intermediate)

First, read the following list of some of the things that were done by different people. The timings are also given.

1. 7.45–8.30 am: Mukesh read a newspaper.
2. 8.30–9.00 am: Anil had breakfast.
3. 9.00–9.30 am: Shefali drove her car to college.
4. 9.00–9.30 am: Meena travelled by train.
5. 10.00–11.00 am: Rakhee wrote letters.
6. 10.00–11.00 am: Waheeda taught class 12.
7. 11.00–12.00 noon: Meenakshi cleaned her flat.
8. 12 noon–1 pm: Rehman attended a meeting.
9. 1.00–2.00 pm: Mukesh and Anil had lunch.
10. 2.00–3.00 pm: Shefali and Waheeda studied in the library.
11. 3.00–3.30 pm: Anita and Shailaja washed clothes.
12. 3.30–4.30 pm: The Board members discussed your plan.
13. 4.30–5.30 pm: Mrs Kapoor typed letters.
14. 6.00–8.00 pm: The Sharmas watched TV.
15. 8.30–9.30 pm: We had dinner.

Now complete the following sentences in past continuous tense.

1. *Mukesh was reading a newspaper at 8.00 am.*
2. Anil .... at 8.45 am.
3. Shefali .... at 9.15 am.
4. Meena .... at 9.20 am.
5. Rakhee .... at 10.30 am.
6. Waheeda .... at 10.45 am.
7. Meenakshi .... at 11.30 am.
8. Rehman .... at 12.30 pm.
9. Mukesh .... at 1.15 pm.
10. Shefali and Waheeda .... at 2.30 pm.
11. Anita and Shailaja .... at 3.15 pm.
12. The Board members .... at 3.45 pm.
13. Mrs Kapoor .... at 5.00 pm.
14. The Sharmas .... at 7.00 pm.
15. We .... at 9.00 pm.

EXERCISE 3 (ADVANCED)

Rewrite the following sentences. Use the correct form of the verb, either the past continuous or the simple past tense.

1. It (begin) to rain while we (play) cricket.
   It began to rain while we were playing cricket.
2. She (watch) TV when I (phone) her.
3. The bus (go) very fast when I (see) him on his scooter.
4. Roma (write) letters when she (hear) a noise outside.
5. She (fall) down while she (cross) the road.
6. I (make) tea while he (sit) in the drawing room.
7. I (see) her at the party. She (wear) a beautiful dress.
8. I (saw) small boats while we (land) at the airport.
9. When I (go) to house, he (take) lunch.
10. The children (play) in the garden when they (see) a strange dog.
11. He (talk) to a client when he (learn) that his mother had passed away.
12. They (do) their morning exercise when they (see) clouds in the sky.
13. Meenakshi (take) our class while it (rain) outside.
14. We (listen to) the evening news when a cat (enter) the room.
15. They (shout) when the Principal entered the classroom.

Unit 16

THE PAST PERFECT AND PAST PERFECT CONTINUOUS TENSES

The Past Perfect Tense

Form

The past perfect tense is formed using *had* and the past participle (*-ed*) form of the main verb.

(1) The plane *had arrived* before they reached the airport.

(2) When I reached school, the English teacher *had already finished* her class.

Uses of the past perfect tense

We usually use the past perfect tense when we talk about two actions in the past. We use the past perfect tense for the event that happened first and the simple past tense for the event that happened second. For example,

The train left the station at 7.15 pm. I was late. I reached the station at 7.30 pm.

(3) The train had left before I reached the station.

Exercise 1 (intermediate)

Rewrite the following sentences. Use the past perfect form of the verbs in brackets.

1. They (already leave) home when I phoned them.
2. My daughter was very happy to visit the zoo because she (never see) a tiger before.
3. Rakesh was not in his office. He (go) to deposit money in bank.
4. After we (eat) dinner, we went out for a walk.
5. I felt that I (see) him somewhere before.
6. The rain (already stop) when I reached Nainital.
7. We were surprised to know that he (build) a large bungalow.
8. The public library was no longer open. It (close) down.
9. When I reached the bus station, I remembered that I (leave) my certificates at home.
10. I couldn't identify my car. It (badly damage)

11. She told me that she (meet) Radhika in the morning.
12. When we reached home, our mother (already prepare) the lunch.
13. I realised that I (meet) her earlier.
14. They went home after they (teach) their classes.
15. I didn't recognise my aunt. She (grow) old.

Exercise 2 (advanced)

Construct sentences using the words in brackets. Use only past perfect tense.

1. She was very happy. (she/get/grade A/in the final examination)
   She had got grade A in the final examination.
2. I reached the station late. (the train/already/leave)
3. He was not in his office when I went to see him there. (he/already/leave/his office)
4. Seema wasn't at home when I arrived. (she/just/go/out)
5. I was late. (the car/break down/on the way)
6. Waheeda couldn't drive the big car. (she/only/drive/small cars earlier)
7. Rehman couldn't attend the party last night. (He/go/to Delhi)
8. Nobody opened the door when I reached their house last night. (probably/everyone/go/to sleep)
9. She didn't have lunch with me yesterday. (she/already/take/her lunch)
10. There was no food left when we reached their house. (the party/already/be/over)

The Past Perfect Continuous Tense

Form

The past perfect continuous tense is formed using *had been + the present participle form of the main verb.*

(4) She *had been waiting* for Michael for four hours before he arrived.

(5) The ground was wet outside when I got up in the morning yesterday. It *had been raining* all through the night.

Uses of the past perfect continuous tense

- We use the past perfect continuous tense to say how long something had been happening before *something else* happened.

(6) Mr Sinha *had been teaching* for thirty-five years in our college before he retired.

- The past perfect continuous tense can also be used to draw conclusions.

(7) The ground was wet outside. It *had been raining* all through the night.

EXERCISE 3 (INTERMEDIATE)

Read the following sentences. Then write a sentence with the help of the words in brackets.

1. She went to college in the morning and came home in the evening. She looked very tired. (she/teach/in college/the whole day).
   She had been teaching in college the whole day.
2. When I saw her, Mukesh was driving his car. (he/drive/his car/since morning).
3. We played cricket for an hour. Then it started raining. (we/play/cricket/for an hour)
4. When I entered the house, I heard the sound of the TV. (someone/watch/TV)
5. When I entered my office, I saw my secretary typing a letter. (my secretary/type/a letter/since morning)
6. My daughter looked very happy as she was reading *Oliver Twist.* (my daughter/read/*Oliver Twist*/since her vacation started.)
7. Rehman started working in Aden in 1986. He was still working in Aden in 1996. (Rehman/work/in Aden/for ten years)
8. When I reached their house, they were eating lunch. (they/eat/lunch)
9. When I entered his office, I found that he was sleeping. (he/sleep/in his office/all afternoon)
10. Two girls came into the classroom. They were all wet. (they/walk/in rain)

EXERCISE 4 (ADVANCED)

Read each situation carefully and then fill in the blanks with appropriate words.

1. We started singing in the main hall. After half an hour the power supply was disrupted.
   We had been singing in the main hall for half an hour when the power supply was disrupted.

2. She was washing clothes in the washing machine, when I reached her house. She .... for an hour when .... her house.
3. I promised to meet her in the library. I went to the library at 2 o'clock. After half an hour I realised that I was in the wrong room. I .... for half an hour when I ....
4. Dr Kapur went to England in 1987. A year later he got a job in a hospital. Dr Kapur .... for a year before he got a job in a hospital.
5. Meenakshi came to the library at 11.30 am and waited for me. I reached the library at 12.00 noon. Meenakshi .... for half an hour before I .... the library.

Unit 17

EXPRESSING FUTURE TIME 1

There are several ways of expressing future time in English; however, the three most common ways of expressing future time are 1. with the modals *will/shall* 2. with *be + going to* and 3. using present continuous tense.

Use of will/shall

- *Will/shall* + the base form of the verb is used to make a prediction of an event on which one does not have any control.
  - (1) He'*ll be* in the office by now.
  - (2) It *will rain* in the evening.

Adverbials such as *tomorrow, next week, next month, next year*, at *2 o'clock, on Friday* etc. can be used with *will/shall.*

Some native speakers use *shall* with *I/we* as the subject and *will* with all other personal pronouns (*you, they, he, she,* etc.).

(3) I *shall take* your class on Monday.

(4) Monica *will take* your class on Monday.

However, some native speakers do not maintain the distinction between *will/shall.*

- Will is also used to express willingness to do something.
  - (5) Don't worry, *I'll drop* you at the station.

Exercise 1 (elementary)

Rewrite the following sentences using *will/shall + the base form* of the verb in brackets.

1. We (stage) a play next month.
2. It (be) a bright day tomorrow.
3. I (drop) you at the bus stand.
4. They (buy) a car next year.
5. I (sell) my house in December.
6. I (send) you a card from Mumbai.
7. The wedding (take place) next Sunday.
8. We (attend) the party, if you invite us.
9. You (get) your degree in September.

10. They definitely (pass) the exam.
11. I (wash) clothes on Sunday.
12. She (go) to the post office on Friday.
13. It (be) very hot in April this year.
14. She (write) to you soon.
15. We (have) a thunderstorm tomorrow.

Exercise 2 (intermediate)

Fill in the blanks with *will/shall* + *the base form* of the verb in brackets.

1. Rajesh: It's raining outside.
   Meena: We .... (stay) inside till it stops raining.
2. Hari: Sorry, I don't have any money.
   Geetha: Don't worry, I .... (pay) for the lunch.
3. Mukesh: Can you take me to the station tonight?
   Rajan: Sure, I .... (take) you to the station as I'm free tonight.
4. Ali: When will you declare the result?
   Mr Kapur: We .... (declare) the result on Monday morning.
5. Seema: Did you post the letter?
   Rakhi: I'm sorry I forgot. I .... (go) to the post office now and post this letter.
6. Rehman: I don't know how to operate this machine.
   Karan: Come, I .... (show) you how to operate this machine.
7. Sarada: What would you have?
   Vinay: I .... (have) some coffee, please.
8. Pramod: What time will you take our class?
   Mr Khanna: I .... (take) your class at 10 o'clock.
9. Beena: Did you phone him?
   Asha: Sorry, I didn't. I .... just (phone) him now.
10. Shefali: When will you have a vacation?
    Varoon: I .... (have) a vacation in May.

Be + going to

Form: One of the ways to express future time is to use *is/am/are* + *going to* + *the first form of the verb.*

(6) They *are going to meet* the Chief Minister tomorrow.

Uses of *be going to*

- The main use of this structure is to express the intention or plans that will be fulfilled in the near or immediate future.

(7) I'm going to watch this film in the evening.
(8) She's going to wash her car.

- This structure may also express that a given happening is inevitable in the future.

(9) This building is going to collapse.
(10) It is going to rain.

Exercise 3 (intermediate)

Rewrite the following sentences using *is/am/are + going to + verb* instead of *intend/intends to + verb* as given in the example sentence.

1. I intend to take a bath today.
   I'm going to take a bath today.
2. They intend to buy a new car.
3. I intend to have eggs at breakfast today.
4. She intends to leave by the afternoon flight.
5. Rakhi intends to teach us today.
6. We intend to write a book on English grammar.
7. They intend to construct a school building.
8. I intend to have my breakfast.
9. He intends to meet the Principal tomorrow.
10. We intend to have a meeting on Monday.
11. I intend to leave this place in an hour.
12. The government intends to increase the taxes.
13. She intends to stay with her grandmother next month.
14. I intend to visit Rekha on Friday.
15. We intend to read *David Copperfield*.

Exercise 4 (intermediate)

With the help of the words within slashes write what you think is going to happen in the following situations.

1. We have a very strong hockey team.
   We/win/ the match. We're going to win the match.
2. The winter has been rather mild.
   It/very hot/this year. ....
3. We are about twenty kms away from Chandigarh. We/reach/ Chandigarh/in half an hour. ....
4. Mukesh has not been working hard before the examination. He/fail/ in the examination. ....

5. This film has a very powerful story and excellent music. It/be/a hit. ....
6. My college starts at 9 am. It is already 8.45 am. It takes me 25 minutes to reach college. I/be/late/for school. ....
7. A man is walking on the road. There is a manhole in front of him and he can't see it. The man/fall/into the manhole. ....
8. There are black clouds in the sky. It/rain/soon. ....
9. You are only wearing a shirt and it is very cold. You/fall/sick. ....
10. The plane is hovering over the airport. It/land/at the airport/soon. ....

The present continuous tense

The present continuous tense can be used to express future with reference to a definite plan, arrangement or programme.

(11) We are starting the French course in November.
(12) The company is holding elections on Sunday.

Exercise 5 (elementary)

Rewrite the following sentences using the present continuous form of the verbs in brackets.

1. The train (leave) at 7 in the evening.
2. The examinations (start) on 7th April.
3. We (go) out in the evening.
4. She (play) table tennis in the afternoon.
5. I (catch) the bus in a few minutes.
6. We (prepare) the timetable tomorrow.
7. I (meet) her at the station.
8. We (have) a party next Sunday.
9. Joginder (get) married next month.
10. I (work) tomorrow morning.
11. He (meet) us in the afternoon.
12. We (go) by car.
13. We (stage) *As You Like It* on Sunday.
14. They (stay) in a hotel in Delhi.
15. S-Net TV (show) 'Sholay' this evening.

The simple present tense

The simple present tense is used for future reference when we are talking about timetables, schedules, etc. These may refer to examinations, train or bus timings, movies, etc.

(13) The bus leaves Lucknow at 6 pm and reaches New Delhi at 8 am the next day.
(14) The movie starts at 3.00 pm.

Exercise 6 (intermediate)

Rewrite the following sentences using the simple present tense of the verbs in brackets.

1. The plane (leave) at 7 in the evening.
2. The second test match (begin) on Tuesday.
3. The examination (start) next Monday.
4. The train (reach) Mumbai at 4 am.
5. The film (start) at 6.00 pm.
6. We (prepare) the question papers on Monday.
7. The vacation (begin) on Friday.
8. The college (open) on 15th July after the summer vacation.
9. I (be) free on Thursday evening.
10. They (be) busy on Monday morning.

Unit 18

EXPRESSING FUTURE TIME 2

Will+be+v-ing

Will and progressive form *(be+v-ing)* can also be used to refer to future actions/events.

Uses:

- We use *will+be+v-ing* to say that we will be in the middle of doing something at a certain time in the future.
  (1) She'll be travelling tomorrow morning.
  (2) We shall be playing football at 4 o'clock on Monday.
- We also use *will+be+v-ing* like the present continuous for planned action.
  (3) I'll be seeing the Vice-chancellor tomorrow.
  (4) I'll be going to Patna on Friday.

Exercise 1 (intermediate)

Rewrite the following sentences using *will+be+v-ing* for the verbs in brackets.

1. He (sleep) at 3 o'clock.
   He'll be sleeping at 3 o'clock.
2. I (watch) TV after dinner.
3. He (dictate) a letter to her in the morning.
4. We (play) football from 4.00 to 5.30 in the evening.
5. I (teach) when you come back.
6. She (work) at 11 o'clock tomorrow.
7. We (clean) the house tomorrow morning.
8. I (travel) next Sunday at this time.
9. They (type) your papers all through the day.
10. We (drive) to Varanasi next Monday morning.
11. She (paint) the house after lunch.
12. I (cooking) lunch after returning from college.
13. He (teach) after attending the meeting.
14. We (bake) biscuits in the afternoon.
15. I (wash) utensils after the party.

EXERCISE 2 (INTERMEDIATE)

Rewrite the following sentences using the *will+be+v-ing* form of the verbs in brackets.

1. I (spend) a week in London.
   I will be spending a week in London.
2. We (hold) the examination in the second week of May.
3. She (meet) us at the airport.
4. We (play) the football match on Saturday.
5. I (sign) all the letters in the afternoon.
6. The plane (leave) in half an hour.
7. The train (arrive) in an hour.
8. We (give) rebate on all items from Monday.
9. They (have) dinner in half an hour.
10. He (see) you in ten minutes.

Will+have+v-en (past participle)

We use *will+have+v-en* to indicate that something will already have happened before a certain time in the future.

(5) I will have completed this book by the end of the year.
(6) The play will have ended by 8 o'clock.

EXERCISE 3 (INTERMEDIATE)

Rewrite the following sentences using *will+have+v-en* for the verbs in brackets.

1. We (construct) the house by the end of the month.
   We will have constructed the house by the end of the month.
2. By the end of next week, they (complete) their training.
3. He (take) the examination by the end of May.
4. By the end of this week, I (wait) for ten weeks for his reply.
5. India (become) a great nation by the end of this decade.
6. She (finish) teaching us French by the beginning of the next month.
7. She (stay) with us for four weeks by next Monday.
8. He (spend) all his money before the end of the holidays.
9. Next year, they (be) in India for five years.
10. By next May, he (write) his next book.

EXERCISE 4 (ADVANCED)

Complete the following sentences.

1. By tomorrow evening, *my parents will have come back home.*
2. By next December, ...
3. By next Sunday ....
4. By the time I finish this book, ...
5. By Monday evening ....

Unit 19

NEGATIVES

We use *not* (*n't*) in negative sentences. We add *not* or *n't* after the state verbs *is, are, was, were* and after the auxiliaries *is, are, was, were, have, had* and after modal auxiliaries *can, could, will, would* etc. After the auxiliaries *are* and *may* only *not* is used.

	Positive	**Negative**
(1)	He *is* a cricket player.	He *is not/isn't* a cricket player.
(2)	They *are* tall.	They *are not/aren't* tall.
(3)	She *is* sleeping.	She *is not/isn't* sleeping.
(4)	They *were* watching TV.	They *were not/weren't* watching TV.
(5)	Vina *has* read this book.	Vina *has not/hasn't* read this book.
(6)	They *can* lift this stone.	They *cannot/can't* lift this stone.
(7)	You *should* do this.	You *should not/shouldn't* do this.
(8)	He *will* see you tomorrow.	He *will not/won't* see you tomorrow.
(9)	I *am* tired.	*I am not tired.*

Notice that one may use the full forms such as *is not, am not, were not* etc. in written English. However, in spoken/oral communication one needs to use the contracted forms such as *isn't, aren't* etc.

Exercise 1 (Elementary)

Change the following sentences into their negative forms.

1. They have finished the work.
2. Her brother is an officer.
3. They are very tall.
4. I am watching TV.
5. She was running fast.
6. We have purchased this house.

7. Asha and Vibha are playing the piano.
8. Mira can fly a plane.
9. Mrs Kapur will teach us tomorrow.
10. We are working right now.
11. Meena and Urmila have spoken to me.
12. You must exercise in the morning.
13. She can speak French.
14. Rajinder and Mohit are studying in the library.
15. They were great singers.
16. I am thirty years old.
17. We could see her from a distance.
18. I would do it.
19. Haridas has cooked the lunch.
20. She is a teacher.
21. Bill and Tom were late.
22. I am very tired.
23. You must sleep outside.
24. Razia has sung this song.
25. The flowers are very attractive.

Negatives with *do not* (don't), *does not* (doesn't) and *did not* (didn't)

In the sentences discussed earlier in this unit, the positive sentence has a state verb, an auxiliary or a modal auxiliary. Therefore, when we change such a positive sentence into its negative form, the negative particle *not* (*n't*) is placed after the state verb, auxiliary or the modal auxiliary. However, look at the following sentences and their negatives.

	Positive	Negative
(10)	I *sleep* in the afternoon.	I *do not (don't) sleep* in the afternoon.
(11)	Rita *studies* in our school.	Rita *does not (doesn't) study* in our school.
(12)	We *attended* the party.	We *did not (didn't) attend* the party.

Here the positive sentences have only main verbs. If a positive sentence has only the main verb, we use *do not* (don't), *does not* (doesn't) or *did not* (didn't) before the base form of the main verb.

- In the simple present tense, we add *do not* (*don't*) if the subject is *I, we, you, they, John and Mary* etc.
- In the simple present tense, we add *does not* (*doesn't*) if the subject is *he, she, it, Rita, John* etc.
- In the simple past tense, we add *did not* (*didn't*) after the subject.

EXERCISE 2 (ELEMENTARY)

Rewrite the following sentences in their negative forms.

1. She takes tea in the morning.
2. I eat rice everyday.
3. They went to the station in the morning.
4. Amitabh and Neeta played tennis yesterday.
5. Raghavan runs very fast.
6. He hit a century yesterday.
7. Our servant cuts vegetables in the evening.
8. We enjoyed the movie.
9. She speaks Italian.
10. They like mangoes.
11. We work here.
12. He signs well.
13. She constructed this house.
14. They go to office in the morning.
15. Rehman and Aziz bought books yesterday.

EXERCISE 3 (ELEMENTARY)

Rewrite the following sentences in their negative forms using the contracted *n't*.

1. My father works in a company.
2. They were running fast.
3. She opened the door.
4. My brother has reached Hyderabad.
5. You must work in the evening.
6. He is a bank manager.
7. The car was expensive.
8. I am taking rest.
9. Her brothers drive.
10. It is hot today.
11. Reena and Arvind have written this article.

12. My sister can drive very fast.
13. She should work at night.
14. We went on vacation last year.
15. It is raining outside.
16. We visited Nainital last summer.
17. My sister has purchased a car.
18. She was speaking to my brother.
19. My uncle owns this shop.

Unit 20

SOME MORE NEGATIVES

Negatives of *have* and *have got*

The most usual way of forming the negative with *have* is to use *do not* (don't), *does not* (doesn't) or *did not* (didn't) before *have.*

	Positive	Negative
(1)	She *has* a book.	She *does not (doesn't) have* a book.
(2)	I *had* my driving license with me.	I *did not (didn't) have* my driving license with me.

However, we add *not* or *n't* after *have* in the case of *have got.*

	Positive	Negative
(3)	She *has got* a book.	She *has not (hasn't) got* a book.
(4)	Sadhana had got her driving license.	Sadhna *had not (hadn't) got* her driving license.

Exercise 1 (intermediate)

Rewrite the following sentences in their negative forms.

1. I have a pet cat.
2. She has a small refrigerator.
3. They had a garage in their compound.
4. Vikram has a good memory.
5. They have excellent books.
6. She has got a lovely garden.
7. Naresh had a cat when he was young.
8. I have got a ticket with me.
9. Monica has enough books to make a library.
10. We keep a dog in our flat.

Exercise 2 (advanced)

Fill in the blanks with a negative verb (*isn't, haven't, don't, can't* etc.).

1. She is short; therefore she .... be a basketball player.
2. I have a red scooter but I .... have a red cycle.

3. It is raining outside. We .... go on a picnic today.
4. Her father walks down to his office. He .... go to his office by bus.
5. Monica's mother .... a doctor; she is a nurse.
6. Where is Shefali? I .... know. I .... seen her today.
7. I .... the pilot of this plane. I am a passenger.
8. I've been to Delhi several times, but I .... been to Mumbai.
9. The office has a vehicle but it .... a driver.
10. 'Would you like to have some cold drink?' 'No, thanks. I .... thirsty.'
11. My uncle .... live in Indira Nagar. He lives in Gomti Nagar.
12. We .... go to Nainital. We went to Ooty during the vacation.
13. When we went to Chandigarh, we stayed with my aunt. We .... stay in a hotel.
14. I .... go to the office yesterday because I .... feeling well. But I'm better now and so I'll go to the office today.
15. She .... play the piano. She plays the violin.
16. I don't like this game. It .... very interesting.
17. My parents .... coming today. They'll come tomorrow.
18. My mother has a house in Hyderabad but she .... a house in Chennai.
19. She was very tired. Therefore she .... play with us in the evening.
20. My brother studied in Modern School. He .... study in DAV Public School.
21. Madhavan .... be here tomorrow. He is leaving for Bangalore tonight.
22. She .... do this work. She is just a child.
23. It is dark outside. I .... see anything.
24. 'Who broke this glass?' I .... know.
25. The children are sitting inside. They .... playing outside.

No or *not + any*

Compare the following sentences.

(5a) He doesn't have any time.
(5b) He has *no time.*

The *not + any* combination is used, when we negate the verb but *no* is usually used before a noun when the verb is not negated.

EXERCISE 3 (ADVANCED)

Rewrite the following sentences with *no*.

1. He doesn't have any money to give you.
   He has no money to give you.
2. I can't see her anywhere.
3. There aren't any books on the table.
4. There wasn't any milk in the fridge.
5. They don't have any fans in the house.
6. Naresh doesn't have any free time.
7. She didn't offer us anything in the evening.
8. There wasn't any servant in the kitchen.
9. He doesn't like any book with sad endings.
10. I'm not going to give him any book.
11. There isn't any coat in the cupboard.
12. I don't have any sugar in the house.
13. He didn't receive any letter yesterday.
14. My uncle can't read anything at night.
15. There aren't any vehicles parked in the porch.

EXERCISE 4 (ADVANCED)

Write the following sentences with *not + any*.

1. There is no salt in the bottle.
   There isn't any salt in the bottle.
2. He has no cars in his office.
3. They have no books with them.
4. I have no stamps.
5. Rita has no brothers or sisters.
6. The little girl had no cotton clothes.
7. There's no petrol in the scooter.
8. There are no mangoes in the basket.
9. Mrs Mehta gave us nothing to drink in the evening.
10. I have no dogs in my house.
11. She has no more thread to give you.
12. There is nobody outside.
13. My sister can read nothing in the evening.
14. My mother has put no sugar in the tea.
15. They will do no work today.

EXERCISE 5 (ADVANCED)

Fill in the blanks with *no* or *any*.

1. There aren't .... books lying on the table.
   There aren't *any* books lying on the table.
2. There are .... apples in the fridge.
3. She didn't leave .... milk in the bowl.
4. He has .... cars in his office.
5. There are .... vacant houses in this building.
6. They don't have .... pencils in their bags.
7. My brother hasn't got .... vehicle.
8. My sister is married, but she has .... children.
9. I don't have .... friends.
10. I have .... friends.
11. There are .... taxis available today.
12. Mrs Chatterjee didn't order .... taxis on Tuesday.
13. I'm sorry there is .... tea left in the kettle.
14. He has .... money left with him.
15. She doesn't have .... money left with her.

Negative statements with negative adverbs

We can make negative statements with adverbs such as *never, hardly, hardly ever, none, seldom* and *rarely.* Compare:

(6a) I *don't eat* mutton.
(6b) I *never eat* mutton.

Notice that *never, hardly* etc. are more emphatic than *not.* Also notice that we can't use a *negative verb* and a negative adverb. It is wrong to say:

(6c) *I don't never eat meat.*

EXERCISE 6 (ADVANCED)

Rewrite the following sentences by using the negative adverb in brackets instead of a negative verb.

1. She doesn't watch TV (never).
   She never watches TV.
2. I'm not going anywhere. (nowhere)
3. She doesn't speak to him. (seldom)
4. We don't meet each other in office. (hardly)
5. She didn't say anything. (nothing)
6. I don't know anyone in this locality. (nobody)

7. We don't know our neighbours. (scarcely)
8. My mother does not visit us very often. (rarely)
9. Mrs Kulkarni can't speak English. (hardly)
10. We don't eat out very often. (rarely)
11. She didn't ever speak to me. (never)
12. I don't drink tea in the morning. (never)
13. Krishna didn't speak to anybody. (nobody)
14. We couldn't sleep at night. (hardly)
15. I don't drive my car. (seldom)
16. My father doesn't go to the cinema. (never)
17. I can't speak to him on the phone. (seldom)
18. We haven't seen her anywhere. (nowhere)
19. Professor Kumar does not take his lectures these days. (scarcely)
20. She has not bought any apples. (no)

Unit 21

YES-NO QUESTIONS

Read the following sentences.

	Positive Sentence	Question
(1)	She is a doctor.	Is she a doctor?
(2)	He was angry.	Was he angry?
(3)	Vinod is sleeping.	Is Vinod sleeping?
(4)	They have finished the work.	Have they finished the work?
(5)	Madhu can sing.	Can Madhu sing?

There is a simple rule to learn here. If a positive sentence has a linking verb *is, am, are, was, were*, or an auxiliary like *is, am, are, was, were, have, has, had*, or a modal auxiliary like *can, could, may, might* etc., we form the question by placing the linking verb, the auxiliary or the modal auxiliary before the subject. Also use the question mark (?) at the end of the sentence.

EXERCISE 1 (ELEMENTARY)

Rewrite the following sentences as questions.

1. Her mother is an army officer.
   Is her mother an army officer?
2. The Principal will be here tomorrow.
3. She has written this book.
4. The children are studying in the hall.
5. He could go on leave next week.
6. My friend will be staying with you.
7. The guests are enjoying the music.
8. He has a dog in his house.
9. She is really ill.
10. They would like an invitation to attend the party.
11. They are on their way here.
12. He has a sister.
13. She must attend the lecture tomorrow.
14. I am late.
15. She is taking a bath.

16. He has a vehicle.
17. They have gone out.
18. He can leave tomorrow.
19. Dr Arvind is at home.
20. Her mother was a teacher.

Read the following sentences.

	Positive Sentence	Question
(6)	She works hard.	Does she work hard?
(7)	The food tastes good.	Does the food taste good?
(8)	They work in a bank.	Do they work in a bank?
(9)	He reached the station on time.	Did he reach the station on time?
(10)	They finished the work yesterday.	Did they finish the work yesterday?

If a positive sentence has a main verb only, we change it into a question by using *do, does* or *did* before the subject.

- We use *does* if the subject is a third person singular (*he, she, it, Rehman* etc.) and the verb is in the simple present tense. We use the base form of the verb in questions.
- We use *do,* if the subject is *I, we, you, they, John* and *Mary* etc. and the verb is in the simple present tense. We use the base form of the verb again.
- We use *did* if the verb is in the past tense. We again use the base form of the verb only.

Exercise 2 (elementary)

Rewrite the following sentences as questions.

1. They work in this office.
   Do they work in this office?
2. Radha finished reading this book yesterday.
3. He drives a car every morning.
4. She sings well.
5. She paid him the money to buy vegetables.
6. It takes a lot of time.
7. Vanit and Pooja go to office by bus.
8. Her father flew a plane on this route.

9. She went to Delhi on Monday.
10. Madhu teaches children in the evening.
11. Sonu and his friend run five miles every morning.
12. They live in Hyderabad.
13. Professor Narayan retired last year.
14. She swims everyday in the evening.
15. Rakesh left a message for her in the evening.
16. Nita and her husband often go for a walk in the morning.
17. Nitin received the General Manager at the station.
18. Mona studies in this college.
19. She runs a mile everyday.
20. They attended her lecture in the afternoon.

Exercise 3 (intermediate)

Write questions with the help of the statements and the words given in brackets.

1. I am reading a novel. (and you?)
   Are you reading a novel?
2. I sleep in the afternoon. (and Seema?)
   Does Seema sleep in the afternoon?
3. I have already seen this film. (and Farida?)
4. I met her in college. (and you?)
5. I like working in a bank. (and you?)
6. I have a dog. (and Pamela?)
7. I'll watch TV tomorrow. (and Rohit?)
8. I was late for the lecture today. (and you?)
9. I can make a doll. (and Meenakshi?)
10. I lived in the centre of the city in Mumbai (and you?)
11. I am waiting for Prashad. (and you?)
12. I can teach you French. (and Swami?)
13. I had a nice holiday. (and you?)
14. I'm going out this evening. (and they?)
15. I could read Sanskrit when I was young. (and you?)
16. I've already taken lunch. (and Promilla?)
17. I'm going to London next month. (and your parents?)
18. I am a pilot. (and Mukesh?)
19. I run five miles everyday. (and you?)
20. I've been to New York recently. (and you?)

EXERCISE 4 (ADVANCED)

Write questions with the help of the following words in brackets. The second bracket has a word/words which can be used as the subject.

1. (a car outside?) (there)
   Is there a car outside?
2. (sleep well last night?) (she)
   Did she sleep well last night?
3. (work in a bank?) (Mohini)
4. (been to Cochin?) (you)
5. (have a pet?) (they)
6. (married?) (you)
7. (like milk?) (he)
8. (break the window yesterday?) (Ramesh)
9. (a doctor?) (your father)
10. (have a refrigerator?) (you)
11. (rain a lot in Shimla?) (it)
12. (very beautiful?) (Rekha)
13. (tall?) (your parents)
14. (watch TV last Monday?) (you)
15. (have a dog in her house?) (she)
16. (meet Iqbal on Monday?) (you)
17. (have finished work?) (they)
18. (live in the USA?) (he)
19. (been a policeman?) (her uncle)
20. (go out last night?) (Prabha)

Yes-no short answers

- We answer the yes-no question by using the pronoun for the subject followed by the auxiliary.
  (11) Is she your cousin? Yes, she is *or* No, she isn't.
  (12) Did he meet you yesterday? Yes, he did *or* No, he didn't.
  (13) Can Rajan do this work? Yes, he can *or* No, he can't.
- We usually do not answer a yes-no question in full or just with *yes* or *no*.

EXERCISE 5 (INTERMEDIATE)

Answer the following questions with short answers. First give your answer with *yes, . . .* and then with *no, ...*

1. Will you teach us tomorrow?
2. Did Amiya give you my book?
3. Have you read this book?
4. Are they sleeping inside?
5. Is it cold outside?
6. Does Vaishali work with you?
7. Have you been to Hyderabad?
8. Is she your cousin?
9. Did they complete the job yesterday?
10. Are you still learning German?
11. Is Maria watching TV?
12. Will you attend the meeting tomorrow?
13. Do they play in the evening?
14. Was she really serious about this project?
15. Would you like to do it?
16. Has he spoken to you about the party?
17. Have you ever eaten fish?
18. Is it hot in the month of March?
19. Did they lock the house?
20. Are they sitting under the sun?
21. Is Annapoorna your English teacher?
22. Will you attend the prize distribution function?
23. Have your parents constructed their house?
24. Do you own this house?
25. Is she really very artistic?

Unit 22

WH-QUESTIONS

In Unit 21, we practised *yes-no* questions. *Yes-no* questions have the answers starting with *yes, . . .* or *no, . . .* The second type of questions is *wh-questions*, which question a particular element of a sentence. A wh-question may question the subject, object, complement, adverbial, verbal etc. of a sentence.

	Positive	**Wh-question**
(1)	*Prakash* wrote this letter.	*Who* wrote this letter? (subject)
(2)	I met *Monisha* at the party.	*Whom* did you meet at the party? (object)
(3)	I saw *'Ben Hur'* yesterday.	*What* did you see yesterday? (object)
(4)	Rekha joined this course *last month*.	*When* did Rekha join this course? (adverbial)

We use the wh-word at the beginning followed by the auxiliary before the subject. If there is no auxiliary in the positive sentence, we use *do, does* or *did*.

(5)	She is going *to Delhi* tomorrow.	*Where* is she going tomorrow?
(6)	He goes to office *by car.*	*How* does he go to office?

However, when the *wh-word* questions the subject, there is no inversion of the auxiliary or there is no use of *do, does* or *did*.

(7)	*Rehman* lives in that house.	*Who* lives in that house?
(8)	*Mira* will attend the meeting.	*Who* will attend the meeting?

Subject questions

We use *who, what, which* or *whose* as the wh-words to question a subject. A subject-question asks for the identity of the subject. There is no inversion of the subject and auxiliary; as such a subject question has the same word order as that of a statement.

		Answer
(9)	*Who* opened the door?	I did.
(10)	*Who* will water the plants?	Rita will.
(11)	*What* has frightened you?	This dog has.
(12)	*Which* boy has done this?	That boy.
(13)	*Whose* dog is barking?	Sheila's.

EXERCISE 1 (ELEMENTARY)

Fill in the blanks with *who, what, which* or *whose*. Sometimes more than one answer is possible. Give all the possible answers.

1. .... is standing under the tree?
2. .... girl wants to play with you?
3. .... book is lying on the table?
4. .... will open this box?
5. .... river flows through Lucknow?
6. .... is lying under your chair?
7. .... is her father's name?
8. .... left the door open?
9. .... film is being shown on the TV today?
10. .... train goes to Bangalore?
11. .... is burning in the kitchen?
12. .... met you in the market yesterday?
13. .... is wrong with her today?
14. .... can lift this couch?
15. .... of these books is yours?
16. .... is your English teacher?
17. .... teaches you history?
18. .... will happen now?
19. .... was speaking in the corridor?
20. .... wants to meet me?
21. .... dog bit you?
22. .... shirt is lying in the corner?
23. .... car is parked outside?
24. .... would like to play badminton?
25. .... will make you happy?

Object questions

We use *who(m), what, which* and *whose* to question an object. In addition, there is inversion of the auxiliary and subject. *Who* is informal and *whom* is formal.

(14) *Who(m)* did you meet at the party?
(15) *What* did she eat at lunch?
(16 *Which* book have you written recently?
(17) *Whose* book have you reviewed recently?

Exercise 2 (intermediate)

Fill in the blanks with *who(m), what, which* or *whose*.

1. .... do you want to meet?
2. .... has done this?
3. .... film did you watch last night?
4. .... film will be telecast tomorrow?
5. .... shall we do now?
6. .... do you want me to do now?
7. .... are you doing in the kitchen?
8. .... did you call yesterday?
9. .... car did you buy at the auction? (Mary's)
10. .... washed the dishes last night?
11. .... did she do last night?
12. .... books can I take home?
13. .... is playing music loudly?
14. .... shirt was she wearing? (Shailaja's)
15. .... does he want?
16. .... shall we do tomorrow?
17. .... scooter is this? Is it yours?
18. .... called you in the morning?
19. .... did you call in the morning?
20. .... car have you sold recently?
21. .... will meet you at the station?
22. .... will you meet at the station?
23. .... dog have you kept in your house? (Usha's)
24. .... happened last night?
25. .... did you do last night?
26. .... did she ring up on her mobile phone?
27. .... is she painting?
28. .... does Kiran like?
29. .... are you reading?
30. .... is reading the newspaper?

Adverbial questions

We use *when, where, why* and *how* to question the adverbial elements of a statement. *When* questions *adverbials of time; where, adverbials of place; why, adverbials of reason;* and *how, adverbials of means/manner.*

(18) They will reach Mumbai *in the morning.*
When will they reach Mumbai?

(19) I met her *at the airport.*
Where did you meet her?

(20) She gave him money *because he was very ill.*
Why did she give him money?

(21) I go to college *by bus.*
How do you go to college?

Exercise 3 (elementary)

Make wh-questions with the help of the following words. Remember to begin with a capital letter and end with a question mark.

1. have you/my keys/kept/where
2. did she/why/go/to Delhi
3. do you/in the morning/when/get up
4. gone/where/has she
5. in class/how/behave/does he
6. teach/can you/when/English/me
7. is the next train/when
8. is my bag /where
9. has he/how/done/in the examination
10. why/attend/did you/the meeting
11. study/did she/when/in this school
12. is the car/parked/where
13. my clothes/where /can I/keep
14. have you/how/it/done
15. can I/when/meet/you
16. did she/why/shout at/you
17. start/acting/when/did you
18. is/Raju/where
19. reach/your home/how/can I
20. will you/your shop/open/when

Exercise 4 (Intermediate)

Rewrite the following statements as *wh-questions* by using a *wh-word* in place of the underlined words.

1. She goes to bed at ten in the evening.
2. He has gone to Kanpur to meet his uncle.
3. He has gone to Delhi.
4. I started going to school when I was four.
5. Mrs Singh will give the lecture at 2 o'clock.
6. She lives in Gomti Nagar.
7. He goes to work by car.
8. She washes her clothes in the washing machine.
9. I'm going to Hyderabad by air.
10. I met her yesterday.
11. They play football in front of their house.
12. They play cricket in the morning.
13. Tarun goes to Indira Nagar to play hockey.
14. I gave him money because he was very poor.
15. She behaves now as if she were a student.
16. She is going to London on Monday.
17. Vaibhav is working very hard these days.
18. Monica met me in the morning.
19. The Director can meet her tomorrow.
20. She would like to work in that room.
21. Rekha is going to Kolkata because her father is ill.
22. Rohin goes for a walk in the morning.
23. He has done the exams quite well.
24. You can ring me up in the afternoon.
25. You can see her in the library.

How + adjective/adverb **can also be used to begin a question.**

(22) *How old* is your father?
(23) *How old* is that building?
(24) *How often* do you go to Chandigarh?

How much + an uncountable noun **can be used to ask about quantity.** ***How much*** **can also be used to ask about cost.**
How many + plural noun **can be used to ask about number.**

(25) *How much* milk is there in the bottle?
(26) *How much* does it cost?
(27) *How many* people attended the party?

Exercise 5 (elementary)

Make *wh-questions* with the help of the following words.

1. do you/for this scooter/How much/want
2. do we/How much/time/have/to get ready
3. is your house/How big
4. is your car/How old
5. cost/How much/does this book
6. in your class/How many/are there/students
7. drink/How many/do you/cups of tea/everyday
8. water/do you/everyday/How much/drink
9. is this plane/How fast
10. is your brother/How tall
11. do you/on vacation/How often/go
12. is the airport/from here/How far
13. attended/How many members/the meeting
14. was the programme/How long
15. is this building/How strong

Exercise 6 (advanced)

Rewrite each of the following statements as a question. Use *how + adjective/adverb/much/many* in place of the underlined word.

1. <u>Fifty</u> people attended the marriage.
2. There is <u>a little</u> milk in the bowl.
3. Her mother is <u>five feet</u> tall.
4. We visit Visakhapatnam <u>every year</u>.
5. There are <u>sixty students</u> in the English literature section.
6. That cloth is <u>five metres</u> long.
7. The Asian Games are held <u>every four years</u>.
8. I want <u>three</u> slices of bread.
9. This book costs <u>fifty rupees</u>.
10. <u>Forty</u> members attended the meeting.
11. I drink <u>five</u> cups of coffee in the morning.
12. There are <u>ten</u> bottles of coke in the fridge.
13. There are <u>twelve</u> inches in a foot.
14. That building is <u>hundred years</u> old.
15. I meet her <u>every day</u>.
16. There is <u>plenty of</u> sugar in the bag.
17. She stayed in England <u>for three years</u>.
18. Her paintings are <u>very</u> good.
19. You have <u>enough</u> time to type this letter.

20. This building is sixty feet high.

Many wh-questions beginning with *who/what/where/which* often end with a preposition (*to/for/about/with* etc.)

(28) Who was she talking to?
(29) What is he interested in?
(30) Where are they from?
(31) Which room is Shikha in?

EXERCISE 7 (INTERMEDIATE)

Turn the following statements into *wh-questions* by replacing the underlined word(s) with an appropriate *wh-word* given within brackets.

1. She was writing with a pen. (what)
2. This scooter belongs to my brother. (who)
3. I'm thinking about your problem. (what)
4. I stayed at a hotel. (which hotel)
5. They are talking about the new programme. (what)
6. He is talking to her uncle. (who)
7. She was sitting in this chair. (which chair)
8. They're going to stay in this hotel. (which hotel)
9. She washed the dishes with this soap. (what)
10. I gave the money to the maid. (who)
11. Avinash was listening to a song. (which song)
12. I'm cutting the vegetables with a knife. (what)
13. I dreamed about my late grandfather. (who)
14. Sadhana is waiting for her driver. (who)
15. They are laughing at a joke. (what)
16. She is from Nepal. (where)
17. My friends are playing with a ball. (what)
18. Usha is talking to our English teacher. (who)
19. He is working for my younger brother these days. (who)
20. Mr Johnson is from Britain. (where)

EXERCISE 8 (INTERMEDIATE)

Rewrite the following statements as *wh-questions*. Replace the underlined word(s) with an appropriate *wh-word*.

1. This is my book.
2. Naresh is reading the newspaper.
3. She gave him some rice in the morning.

4. She has eaten the apple.
5. Vinay and Manoj are playing cricket in the ground.
6. Naresh and Rita are in the library.
7. I met your uncle in the morning.
8. You can meet the Principal tomorrow.
9. They took their rain coats with them as it was raining.
10. My father is seventy years old.
11. She gave him three pens.
12. There is plenty of water in the tank.
13. I visit this temple every month.
14. Twenty members have already come.
15. There are ten boys in the classroom.
16. Mohinder was with Nalini.
17. He is interested in that girl.
18. She is looking at that picture.
19. Mr Khan is the new physics teacher.
20. That girl wants to meet the Principal.
21. This bus goes to Ludhiana.
22. She spoke to her grandmother in the morning.
23. Something happened in the morning.
24. He wants to meet the Director.
25. She behaves very well now.
26. They're sitting under the trees.
27. This is Rahul's shop.
28. The new manager will join for duty on Monday.
29. She has gone to Kathmandu to join a new company.
30. The lunch was very good.
31. We eat very often in this shop.
32. I need little water to have a bath.
33. There is plenty of flour in the bag.
34. She is looking at something.
35. He was afraid of ghosts.

Unit 23

QUESTION TAGS

A question tag is a short question such as *is she?* or *isn't she?* that is used at the end of a statement. It is usually used to confirm a statement.

(1) Her mother is a doctor, *isn't she*?
(2) She can do this job, *can't she*?
(3) Ramesh attended the meeting yesterday, *didn't he*?
(4) Jane hasn't finished the work, *has she*?
(5) They didn't watch TV last night, *did they*?

There are basically two forms of question tags.

Negative statement + positive tag

In this case, we use the auxiliary of the negative statement followed by the appropriate pronoun.

(6) Monica isn't very tall, *is she*?
(7) They don't work in a bank, *do they*?

Positive statement + negative tag

(8) Monica is very tall, *isn't she*?
(9) They work in a bank, *don't they*?

Notice that in sentence (9), the statement doesn't have an auxiliary, so we have used *don't*. We usually use the falling pitch (intonation) (↓) when we speak the question tag.

(10) She won't attend the party, ↓ *will she*?

When the speaker uses the falling intonation, it means that the statement is true. On the other hand, sometimes we may use the question tag with a rising voice (intonation) (↑) if we are less sure of the statement.

(11) Vikas is in the library, ↑ *isn't he*?

Exercise 1 (Advanced)

Use an appropriate negative question tag after each statement.

1. This book is very interesting.
2. The library closes at eight o'clock.

3. Monica and Nalini will arrange the party.
4. It is a big hall.
5. She speaks German fluently.
6. Amrita has painted this picture.
7. They played tennis last evening.
8. Mrs Arora is teaching physics in the main hall.
9. Ravi has gone out.
10. It was a great show.
11. You work here.
12. The train leaves at six o'clock.
13. We can sit under the trees.
14. The food looks good.
15. Shankar would do it.
16. You have got a vehicle.
17. She was at home yesterday.
18. He sang a song at the party.
19. Professor Mahajan gave a lecture in the morning.
20. The summer has been very hot.
21. The book is lying on the table.
22. They went out for a walk in the evening.
23. You are Astha's cousin.
24. The examination will be held next week.
25. He's quite happy.
26. This dog looks fierce.
27. He loves acting.
28. They have lived here for a long time.
29. Your grandmother is sleeping inside.
30. You painted it yourself.
31. Priya has written a novel.
32. We must hurry.
33. Shefali should try again.
34. She prefers tea at breakfast.
35. They drank milk in the morning.

Exercise 2 (advanced)

Use an appropriate positive question tag after each negative statement.

1. Mr Khanna isn't at home.
2. Devi can't speak Hindi.
3. They didn't attend the meeting in the morning.

4. You haven't read this novel.
5. You won't go to Warangal tomorrow.
6. Bill doesn't work in your college.
7. It isn't raining outside.
8. This dog isn't fierce.
9. They couldn't speak to the President.
10. I needn't say anything.
11. He shouldn't eat too much sugar.
12. They weren't at the beach.
13. Your aunt isn't working in the library.
14. I didn't trouble you.
15. You don't want to marry her.
16. Monisha wasn't at home.
17. Neelima doesn't work hard.
18. They haven't paid the rent.
19. Mr Sharma hasn't got a son.
20. She hasn't lived here long.
21. Varinder isn't very old.
22. Zarina wasn't angry.
23. She doesn't believe Rohit.
24. They don't sleep in the afternoon.
25. Rajneesh won't be late.
26. You aren't working on this project.
27. This machine doesn't work.
28. We don't have to pay.
29. Meenakshi couldn't have prevented it.
30. There weren't any tigers in the zoo.
31. Sarita doesn't know you.
32. Mohit and Neena didn't attend the wedding.
33. He isn't furious.
34. Rehman didn't meet her.
35. It isn't your coat.

Question tags with imperatives

After an imperative, we may use either *won't you* or *will you.*

(12) Open the window, *won't you*?
(13) Open the window, *will you*?

Won't you is least insistent and *will you* is most insistent. Though it is possible to use *will you* after a negative imperative, we usually don't use a tag after a negative imperative.

(14) Don't make a noise, *will you*?

We use *shall we*? as a tag after the first person plural imperative beginning with *Let's* . . .

(15) Let's play in the ground, *shall we*?

EXERCISE 3 (ADVANCED)

Use question tags at the end of the following sentences.

1. Wait for me here.
2. Close the door.
3. Don't play here.
4. Let's go out tonight.
5. Give it to me in writing.
6. Don't do it again.
7. Let's watch TV in the hall.
8. Let's discuss it now.
9. Don't be late for the dinner.
10. Pass on the salt, please.

EXERCISE 4 (ADVANCED)

Use an appropriate question tag at the end of each sentence.

1. It was an interesting film.
2. He didn't come home yesterday.
3. You have taken your pay cheque.
4. The plane leaves at five in the morning.
5. Sudha can't read Tamil.
6. You won't come to college tomorrow.
7. Let's go out for lunch tomorrow.
8. Don't drive fast.
9. Her father will meet the Chief Minister tomorrow.
10. These shirts are lovely.
11. She doesn't sweep the room every day.
12. Mona couldn't finish the lesson.
13. Chain the dog.

14. Get me a glass of water.
15. Neha met you in the morning.
16. Professor Kapur is sitting in the staff room.
17. Let's watch this film.
18. These sandwiches look good.
19. Mira could complete this work.
20. She hasn't gone to college today.
21. Place it over there.
22. She dropped him at the railway station.
23. They won't attend the conference.
24. You've been on a holiday.
25. You're Kareena's friend.

Unit 24

ADJECTIVES AND THEIR ORDER

An adjective usually describes a noun and it is used either before a noun or after a linking verb. Examples: *small, beautiful, interesting, old, tired*, etc.

(1) That *tall* boy is a cricket player. (*tall* modifies *boy*)

(2) Her mother is very *tall*. (*tall* is used after *the linking verb*)

(3) It was a *bright* day. (*bright* modifies *day*)

Notice that an adjective can be modified by an adverb, e.g. an *extremely beautiful* girl, an *immensely popular* novel, a *very useful* book.

EXERCISE 1 (INTERMEDIATE)

Fill in the blanks with appropriate adjectives.

1. I saw a .... plane at the airport yesterday.
2. The weather is .... today.
3. We went to a .... place yesterday.
4. That .... boy is my cousin.
5. She is very ....
6. Those .... flowers were given to her at the reception.
7. There is a very .... temple in this town.
8. Drive carefully. There is a .... ditch ahead.
9. He seemed ....
10. The music sounded ....
11. The movie was ....
12. Their .... house is at the back of this building.
13. My .... brothers are army officers.
14. His mother was very ....
15. She is a .... lady.
16. My .... suit is very ....
17. There is an .... man waiting for you outside.
18. His handwriting is very ....
19. They were ....
20. She is driving a .... scooter.
21. His .... car is parked outside.

22. Their .... daughter is getting married to a doctor.
23. Dr Badal is ....
24. They have given me .... clothes.
25. The .... shoes are very ....

EXERCISE 2 (INTERMEDIATE)

Carefully choose the adjectives in box A and nouns in box B and then fill in the blanks with adjective + noun.

A	B
big expensive dangerous high dark elder fresh heavy old beautiful long foreign new difficult	problem book clouds hotels turn wall house air box photographs gift journey languages brother car

1. It's going to rain. There are .... in the sky.
2. Her younger brother is a doctor and her .... is a pilot.
3. My grandfather was a very rich man. He owned a ....
4. Could you open the window? We need some ....
5. She has an old car and she is going to buy a .... next week.
6. Her father gave her an .... on her birthday.
7. He teaches in a language institute, where .... are taught.
8. They are very rich. They stay in ....
9. They've gone on a .... to Kashmir.
10. He is a good photographer. He always takes ....
11. It is an .... He bought it in 1975.
12. There is a .... around their house.
13. He couldn't solve it as it was a ....
14. You can't lift it as it is a ....
15. Drive carefully. There is a .... on the left.

Sometimes a noun may modify another noun, thus functioning as an adjective.

(4) I bought a *cotton shirt* yesterday.

(5) The *film industry* has produced some very good films this year.

EXERCISE 3 (ELEMENTARY)

Fill in the blanks with one of the nouns given below.

tennis steel, garage, chemistry, apple, village, insurance, brick, entertainment, morning, cricket, music, iron, copper, wire

1. She left Mumbai by the .... train.
2. She is a good singer. She has recently opened a .... institute.
3. The .... jug is lying in the kitchen.
4. The electricity company has used .... wires.
5. I couldn't park the car inside last night as the .... door was locked.
6. The .... sarpanch wants to see you.
7. There has been a match-fixing scandal against the .... team.
8. Vibha has submitted her claim to the .... company.
9. As there are many new singers, the .... industry is making a lot of money.
10. The .... houses are quite strong.
11. Our neighbour's daughter has got admission in the .... department.
12. We always had apples at home as we had .... trees all around our house.
13. Karan hit the dog with an .... rod.
14. Steffi Graf was one of the top .... players.
15. They've constructed a .... fence around their house.

Types of adjectives

We can divide adjectives into three types:

- Qualitative adjectives

  These adjectives identify a quality that a person, an animal or a thing has: *happy, tall, beautiful, small, big, tiny.* For example:

  happy girl   *small* cake
  tall boy   *big* dog
  beautiful flower   *tiny* bird

- Classifying adjectives

  These adjectives place a noun in a particular class that it belongs to. Classifying adjectives are words like *central, direct, medieval, golden, international, regional.* For example:

  the *central* government   the *golden* casket
  the *direct* flight   a *regional* issue

- Colour adjectives: Adjectives referring to colour are called colour adjectives.

  brown shoes   *dark brown* hair
  black eyes   *light blue* shirt

When two or more adjectives of different types are used before a noun, the usual order is:

qualitative adjective + colour adjective + classifying adjective + noun. For example:

a *large brown wooden* table — the *new central* government
her *small blue* eyes — his *small black digital* watch

Exercise 4 (advanced)

Put the following words in the right order to make phrases.

1. box, a, metallic, white, little
2. calm, the, wind, Western
3. the, political, party, new
4. cat, a, black
5. an, painting, English
6. heavy, a, vehicle, commercial
7. a, dress, blue, beautiful
8. new, car, a, blue
9. an, ugly, shirt, green
10. the, equipment, agricultural, new
11. Kashmiri, red, a, delicious, apple
12. famous, building, the, Victorian
13. the, regime, weak, military
14. old, an, Hindi, movie
15. successful, the, national, party

Unit 25

DEGREES OF ADJECTIVES

An adjective has comparative and superlative forms.

	Comparative	**Superlative**
high	higher	highest
old	older	oldest
cheap	cheaper	cheapest

(1) It isn't *cold* today. It was *colder* yesterday.
(2) This city is not very *old*. Lucknow is an *older* city.
(3) This is the *highest* peak in this state.
(4) Madhya Pradesh is the *biggest* state in India.

- We use *-er* and *-est* normally after short adjectives with one syllable. We use *more* and *most* before long adjectives with 2/3/4 syllables:

	Comparative	**Superlative**
expensive	more expensive	most expensive
beautiful	more beautiful	most beautiful

(5) Meena is the *most beautiful* girl in our class.
(6) Our dresses are *expensive* but their dresses are *more expensive*.

- We use *-er* and *-est* with two-syllable adjectives ending in *-y:*

	Comparative	**Superlative**
heavy	heavier	heaviest
dirty	dirtier	dirtiest

- There are a few adjectives which have irregular forms:

	Comparative	**Superlative**
good	better	best
bad	worse	worst
far	farther	farthest

EXERCISE 1 (INTERMEDIATE)

Fill in the blanks by using a comparative form of the adjective underlined.

1. People living in cities are not very healthy these days. In the past they were healthier.
2. She doesn't have a big pressure cooker. She wants to purchase a .... cooker now.
3. These mangoes are not very tasty. Those mangoes are ....
4. This flat is modern. She likes .... flats.
5. My sofa isn't very soft. That one is ....
6. This stool isn't very comfortable. That one is ....
7. Her idea wasn't very good. Your idea was ....
8. Her sister isn't very tall. Your sister is ....
9. Monica is tall but Shweta is ....
10. She is very polite but her husband is ....
11. Vikas is quite careful but his son is ....
12. My bag isn't very heavy. Your bag is ....
13. Rakesh was quite helpful but his brother was ....
14. This brush is quite big but I need a .... one.
15. These paintings aren't very pretty. Those paintings are ....

We may use *than* after the comparative form of an adjective.

(7) Meera is *taller than* Vanita.
(8) Delhi is *colder than* Mumbai these days.
(9) She is *older than* her sister.

EXERCISE 2 (INTERMEDIATE)

Read the sentences given below. With the information, construct new sentences. Use the comparative form of the adjectives followed by *than*.

1. Rani is tall but her sister isn't very tall.
   Rani is taller than her sister.
2. Devi is not very musical but Meera is very musical.
   Meera is more musical than Devi.
3. Jammu is hot but Delhi is very hot in summer.
4. Her work is careless but my work is not so careless.
5. Her house is very old but my house isn't very old.
6. His room is very cold but your room isn't very cold.
7. Monish is very quick but Naresh is not so quick.
8. This house is very big but that house is not so big.
9. A car is very expensive but a scooter isn't very expensive.
10. She was very famous but her brother wasn't famous.
11. Meenakshi is a good swimmer but her daughter isn't a good swimmer.

12. My driving is very bad but my wife's driving is not so bad.
13. She is very friendly but her sister is not so friendly.
14. This sum is very simple but the sum given in the book is not so simple.
15. This car is very noisy but your car is not so noisy.
16. Her father was very courageous but her uncle was not so courageous.
17. The major was very brave but the captain was not so brave.
18. My uncle is very wise but my aunt is not so wise.
19. He is very reserved but his sister isn't reserved.
20. This iron bucket is very heavy but that plastic bucket is not so heavy.

We may use *a little/a little bit/much* before the comparative form of an adjective. If the difference between two people, objects etc. is very little, we use *a little/a little bit*. If the difference is large or great, we use *much*.

(10) India is *much bigger* than Sri Lanka.

(11) Sunita is *a little bit taller* than her sister. Sunita is 163 cm tall and her sister is 160 cm tall.

EXERCISE 3 (ADVANCED)

Complete the sentences with *a little/a little bit/much*+the *comparative* + *than* . . . .

1. Delhi has 7° celsius minimum temperature today. Lucknow has 6° celsius minimum temperature today.
   Lucknow is a little colder than Delhi today.
2. Rita is 40 years old and her sister is 20 years old.
   Rita is much older than her sister.
3. My father is 178 cm tall but my uncle is only 155 cm tall. My father is ....
4. Your room is 3 m wide and my room is 2 m 95 cm wide. Your room is ....
5. My uncle is 68 years old and my aunt is only 48 years old. My uncle is ....
6. Rita is meticulous but her sister is extremely meticulous. Rita's sister is ....
7. Yesterday I was very tired but today I don't feel very tired. Yesterday I was ....
8. This book costs Rs 150 and that book costs Rs 145. This book is ....

9. My brother is 30 years old and his wife is 29 years old. My brother is ....
10. A motorcycle costs Rs 40,000 but a car costs at least Rs 200,000. A motorcycle is ....

As mentioned earlier, the superlative form of an adjective is used with *-est* for shorter words and with *most* for longer words.

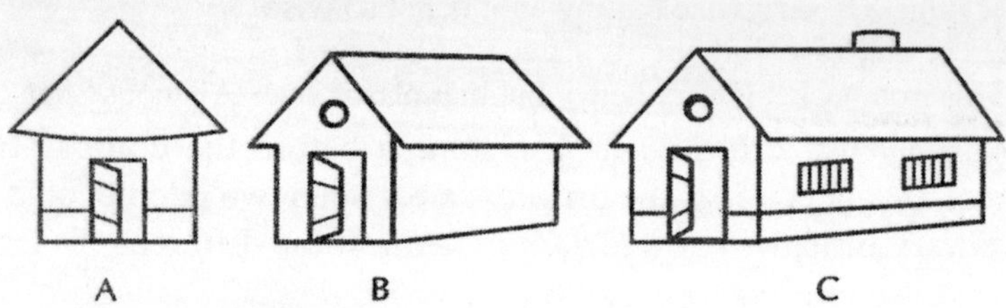

(12a) House B is *bigger* than house A.
(12b) House C is *bigger* than house B.
(12c) House C is the *biggest* house.

Exercise 4 (intermediate)

Complete the following sentences using the superlative form of the adjective.

1. That girl is very tall. *She's the tallest girl in the class.*
2. Madhya Pradesh is a very big state. Madhya Pradesh is .... in India.
3. She's a very talented actress. She's .... in India.
4. It's a very interesting book. It's .... I've ever read.
5. Raghav is a very good student. Raghav is .... in the class.
6. He's a very short boy. He's .... in our team.
7. It's a very old building. It's .... in the city.
8. She's a very diligent girl. She's .... in our college.
9. Vikram is a very brave officer. Vikram is .... in our unit.
10. My aunt is a very kind lady. My aunt is .... I've ever known.
11. He's a very practical man. He's .... in our town.
12. It's a very difficult problem. It's .... in this book.
13. He's a very courageous boy. He's .... in our team.
14. He's a very fast runner. He's .... in our school.
15. She's a very active worker. She's .... in the party.

Exercise 5 (advanced)

Read the following sentences. Rewrite each one with the same meaning. Use a superlative form and the words already given.

1. I've never seen such a stout man. *He's the stoutest man I've ever seen.*
2. I've never met such a tall girl. She's ....
3. I've never seen such a white flower. That's .... seen.
4. I've never eaten such a delicious cake. It's .... eaten.
5. I've never solved such an easy sum. It's .... solved.
6. I've never seen such a beautiful city. This is .... seen.
7. I've never travelled on such a fast train. This is .... travelled on.
8. I've never met such a noble person as Mr Kapur. Mr Kapur's .... met.
9. I've never met such a wise man as you. You're .... met.
10. I've never seen such a red chilly. This is .... seen.
11. I've never eaten such tasty food. It's .... eaten.
12. I've never had such a wonderful dinner. It's .... had.
13. I've never seen such a thin girl as Veena. Veena's .... seen.
14. I've never read such a good story. This is .... read.
15. I've never met such a generous person as Rajan. Rajan's .... met.

Unit 26

PARTICIPLE ADJECTIVES AND FUNCTIONS OF ADJECTIVES

PARTICIPLE ADJECTIVES

There are a large number of adjectives in English which have *-ing* or *-ed* forms and are called *participle adjectives.*

this *amazing* picture:	This picture is *amazing.*
the *shocking* news:	The news was *shocking.*
that *bored* student:	That student feels *bored.*

Some of the *-ing* adjectives are:
amusing, annoying, astonishing, boring, charming, confusing, depressing, disgusting, disturbing, dying, interesting, pleasing, refreshing, shocking, sickening.

Some of the *-ed* adjectives are:
alarmed, amazed, amused, annoyed, armed, bored, confused, convinced, concerned, depressed, disappointed, disgusted, dried, embarrassed, established, frightened, furnished, interested, infected, irritated, pleased, paid, shocked, surprised, trained.

- We often use adjectives with *-ing* endings to describe things or events or what effect it has on us.
  (1) The film was *boring.*
  (2) Our aunt told us an *amusing* story.
- We often use adjectives with *-ed* endings to describe how people feel.
  (3) I felt *bored* while travelling by train.
  (4) She was a *neglected* child in her childhood.

EXERCISE 1 (INTERMEDIATE)

Fill in the blanks with the correct adjective in brackets.

1. The book is so .... that I've already read it three times. (interesting/interested)
2. She felt so .... that she left the room. (boring/bored)

3. It was .... to know that she had failed in the examination. (disturbing/disturbed)
4. My father was .... with her. (annoying/annoyed)
5. We got the .... news of her death, while we were in Singapore. (shocking/shocked)
6. The plane turned to the left sharply. All of us were absolutely .... (terrifying/terrified)
7. I was .... to know that she had failed in the examination. (disturbing/disturbed)
8. My mother was .... by the presence of her aunt. (embarrassing/embarrassed)
9. It was a .... experience to see the plane turning to the left sharply. (terrifying/ terrified)
10. The journey was .... (tiring/tired)

Syntactic Functions of Adjectives

Attributive and predicative: The most frequent use of an adjective or an adjective phrase is either as the modifier before the noun head or as subject complement or object complement. When adjectives occur as prenominal modifiers, they are called *attributive adjectives.* For example,

a *small* boat a *tall* girl

Adjectives functioning as subject complement or object complement are called *predicative adjectives.*

(5) Vanita is *artistic.*
(6) I find Vanita *artistic.*

Most adjectives can be used either in the attributive or predicative position. However, there are a few adjectives which are restricted to either the attributive or predicative position.

Attributive only

the *main* story	not	the story is *main*
utter nonsense	not	the nonsense is *utter*
a *little* cottage		my *monthly* salary
a *pure* thriller		the *only* occasion
a *simple* truth		a *criminal* lawyer
a *true* scholar		

my *old* friend (notice that in *my friend is old*, 'old' has a different meaning)

Predicative only

(7) All of us were *asleep.*	*not*	the *asleep* man
(8) The maid was *unwell.*	*not*	the *unwell* maid
(9) The girl felt *glad.*	*not*	the *glad* girl
(10) The dog is *alive.*	*not*	the *alive* dog

Many adjectives which have complements after them can only be used in the predicative position.

(11) I am *aware* of the danger.
(12) She is *prone* to ill health.
(13) He is *fond* of her.
(14) I am *willing* to do it.
(15) They are *unable* to help you.

Some of the *adjectives/-ed participles* that are followed by a complement are: *afraid, amused, angry, annoyed, answerable, ashamed, convinced, delighted, fond, furious, good, happy, hopeless, liable, pleased, proud, reasonable, sorry, sure, surprised.*

Exercise 2 (advanced)

Make sentences with the adjectives given below. State whether each has been used in the attributive or predicative position.

weekly	unwilling	fond	tired
afraid	eastern	incapable	elder
tall	occasional	thin	anxious
wonderful	glad	daily	pleased
answerable	delighted	liable	wide

Exercise 3 (advanced)

Rewrite the following sentences. Use the *adjectives* given within brackets, along with a suitable preposition.

1. She didn't like his behaviour. (shocked)
   She was shocked at his behaviour.
2. My father plays cricket very well. (good)
3. Monica doesn't like dogs. (afraid)
4. There is enough sugar in the bag. (full)
5. Vijay wants to study literature. (interested)

6. Lata Mangeshkar has sung many songs. (famous)
7. She can't do anything. (incapable)
8. My son has stood first in his class. (proud)
9. Her daughter has failed in the examination. (upset)
10. She can't draw anything. (hopeless)
11. I know Nina doesn't have enough money. (sorry)
12. It's already 10 o'clock. Your school begins at 9.50 am. (late)
13. He can do this work. (fit)
14. He used unkind words while talking to the clerk. (rude)
15. They're waiting for the news. (anxious)

Exercise 4 (advanced)

Rewrite the following sentences using the adjective + infinitive given in brackets.

1. Mohan doesn't want to open the door. (afraid to)
   Mohan is afraid to open the door.
2. He can do it. (able to...)
3. I know that she has passed the examination. (happy to...)
4. This window doesn't open. (difficult to...)
5. She has gone out in the cold with a coat. (stupid to...)
6. I can't drive this car. (unable to...)
7. Karan will definitely pass this examination. (certain to...)
8. Avinash reacts slowly. (slow to...)
9. Shailaja spends so much foolishly. (foolish to...)
10. She draws pictures carefully. (careful to... neatly)
11. I'm sorry because I'm late. (sorry to...)
12. She liked receiving your letter. (overjoyed to...)
13. He very much wants to do this work. (eager to...)
14. He doesn't want to take up this job. (reluctant to...)
15. We will definitely win the match. (sure to...)

Unit 27

ADVERBS 1

Adverbs usually answer questions such as how? how often? when? where? and why?

ADVERBS OF MANNER

- Adverbs of manner tell us *how* something happens.
  (1) She plays *slowly.*
  (2) It rained *heavily.*
- We usually form adverbs of manner by adding *-ly* to an adjective.
  slow ⟶ slowly heavy ⟶ heavily
- After a consonant, *-y* changes to *-i*.
  happy ⟶ happily
- There are some irregular adverbs, which are used without *-ly.*
  (3) She works *hard.*
  (4) She sings *well.*

EXERCISE 1 (INTERMEDIATE)

Fill in the blanks with an appropriate adverb. Use the underlined adjective after changing it into an adverb.

1. She is a good dancer.
   She dances well.
2. He gave an intelligent reply.
   He replied intelligently.
3. Rakesh is a fast runner. He runs ....
4. He gave an informal talk. He talked to us ....
5. The plane was high in the sky. The plane flew ....
6. He is a strange man. He behaves ....
7. She was a foolish woman. She always talked ....
8. We have bought an automatic washing machine. It switches off ....
9. He is a quick reader. He read the book ....

10. The train was <u>late</u>. It arrived ....
11. He was a <u>brave</u> soldier. He fought .... during the war.
12. She was very <u>unhappy</u>. She always talked ....
13. They gave a <u>bad</u> performance. They sang ....
14. He is a <u>slow</u> runner. He runs ....
15. She is a <u>graceful</u> dancer. She dances ....

ADVERBS/ADVERBIALS OF TIME

- Adverbs of time are used to indicate when something *happens, happened* or *will happen*. Some of these adverbs are *now, then, soon* etc. However, the most frequently used adverbials are *today, yesterday, this/next/last week, on Tuesday, at 10 o'clock* etc. Notice that *today, yesterday, this week* etc. are nouns in form but adverbials in function. Similarly, *on Tuesday* and *at 10 o'clock* are prepositional phrases in form but adverbials in function.

  (5) Meera didn't have a TV set *then.*
  (6) He'll come *here soon.*
  (7) I talked to her *last night.*
  (8) You can ring me up *at 6 o'clock in the evening.*

EXERCISE 2 (ELEMENTARY)

Answer the following questions. Use the adverbs/adverbials within brackets.

1. When does she watch TV? *(in the evening)*
   She watches TV in the evening.
2. When did you see her? (yesterday) ....
3. When will she come? (soon) ....
4. When does he get up? (at 5 o'clock) ....
5. When will you ring her up? (tomorrow in the evening) ....
6. When can I meet you? (on Wednesday in the afternoon) ....
7. When did you read this novel? (last month) ....
8. When do the examinations begin? (on 1st March) ....
9. When will you teach us Shakespeare? (now) ....
10. When will you reach Delhi? (Friday morning) ....
11. When did she get the Filmfare award? (in 1992) ....
12. When did she arrive? (Sunday night) ....
13. When was this house constructed? (in 1931) ....

14. When did he join your office? (last year) ....
15. When is she opening her shop? (next month) ....

- *Just, already, yet* and *recently* are used as adverbs with the present perfect tense.

  (9) She has *already* seen this film.
  (10) He hasn't come *yet.*

- *Still* and *not...anymore* are used with the simple present or the present continuous tense.

  (11) She is *still* trying to finish the work.
  (12) He is not working there *anymore.*
  (13) He doesn't work there *anymore.*

Exercise 3 (advanced)

Fill in the blanks with *just, already, yet, recently, still* or *anymore*.

1. She has .... left for home. She must .... be on her way home.
2. I've .... cleaned the shelf. But it .... looks dirty.
3. He took some books from the library last month. He has not .... returned them.
4. Maria is .... having her lunch but her sister has .... finished it.
5. Rakesh doesn't work here .... He has .... joined a bank.
6. My father doesn't own a car .... He has .... sold his old one.
7. I've .... bought a new jeep. I haven't driven it ....
8. She isn't painting ....
9. It's .... raining outside.
10. She hasn't .... spoken to him.

Exercise 4 (advanced)

Rewrite the sentences with an appropriate adverb of time.

1. I have finished reading this book. *I have just finished reading this book.*
2. They are playing football. ....
3. Have you finished eating? ....
4. We watched this film. ....

5. I read this book. ....
6. They played football. ....
7. This machine is not working. ....
8. They have sold their house. ....
9. I met her. ....
10. She left Mumbai. ....
11. She has left Mumbai. ....
12. He is sleeping inside. ....
13. She is not teaching in this college. ....
14. He doesn't work in this bank. ....
15. She doesn't play hockey. ....

- Some adverbs/adverbials like the following can be used with both the simple past and the present perfect tenses: *today, this month, this year.*

(14) I (saw/have seen) him (today/this month/this year)

Exercise 5 (intermediate)

Change the following sentences which are in the present perfect tense into the past tense and vice versa.

1. I saw this film only this month.
2. Have you read the *India Today* this week?
3. I've read the newspaper today.
4. I haven't watched TV today.
5. I spoke to her several times this month.
6. I've written several letters this week.
7. He didn't do anything this year.
8. She hasn't withdrawn the money from the bank today.
9. She didn't clean her car this week.
10. We didn't get water today.

Unit 28

ADVERBS 2

Adverbs of Frequency

Adverbs of frequency generally answer the question *how often*? The adverbs of frequency that are most often used are: *always, almost always, generally, usually, often, frequently, occasionally, sometimes, never.*

Adverbs of frequency occur in a fixed order in a sentence relative to the verb phrase

- after the linking verb *be*.

    (1) She is *generally* late.

- before the main verb, when there is only the main verb.

    (2) He *never* visited us.

- after the auxiliary when there is one.

    (3) I have *never* been late.

- after the first auxiliary when there is more than one.

    (4) He may always have been rude to his students.

Exercise 1 (intermediate)

Rewrite each of the following sentences using the adverb of frequency given within brackets.

1. She visits us. (sometimes)
   She sometimes visits us.
2. I have visited this school. (often)
3. I bring work from the office. (usually)
4. He has been writing a short story. (occasionally)
5. Monica looks bright. (always)
6. Do you work hard? (usually)
7. They have been working late. (frequently)
8. She gets good marks in English. (almost always)
9. She can be rude. (occasionally)
10. Have you lived in this house? (always)

We can also use adverbs of frequency in negative statements.

- The following adverbs are used after *not: always, generally, usually, often.*

  (5) She doesn't *always* cook dinner.

- We may use *generally, normally, often* and *usually* after the subject for special emphasis.

  (6) We *normally* don't work in the evening.

- We use *sometimes* and *frequently* before *not* or after *isn't, doesn't, didn't,* etc.

  (7) She is *sometimes* not very articulate.

  (8) She isn't *sometimes* very articulate.

Exercise 2 (intermediate)

Rewrite the following sentences using the adverbs given within brackets.

1. She wasn't late when she worked in our office. (often)
   She wasn't often late when she worked in our office.
2. She isn't at home in the evening. (usually)
3. He doesn't work in the afternoon. (normally)
4. They didn't complain about the hostel food. (generally)
5. We don't worry if the train is late. (normally)
6. She's not in office when I ring her up. (sometimes)
7. They don't play in the morning. (sometimes)
8. She wouldn't finish the work in time. (often)
9. She doesn't reach home by 10 o'clock. (frequently)
10. Trains aren't very reliable. (always)

Adverbs of Place

One-word adverbs of place are words like *away, there, somewhere, here, anywhere,* etc.

(9) They went *away.*

(10) I've kept it *there/somewhere.*

There are a large number of prepositional phrases that can function as adverbials of place.

(11) She was standing *under the tree.*

(12) They were sitting *in the room.*

Exercise 3 (intermediate)

Fill in the blanks with an adverb/adverbial of place.

1. She was singing ....
2. We found the keys ....
3. She went ....
4. We saw him ....
5. The dog sat ....
6. They live ....
7. She was born ....
8. My father works ....
9. The book is lying ....
10. My mother is cooking lunch ....
11. She teaches ....
12. She is writing a letter ....
13. I met him ....
14. He sang a song ....
15. Tom was sleeping ....

Adverbs of Degree

Adverbs of degree can be used before adjectives or other adverbs to convey information about the degree or extent of something.

(13a) She's happy.
(13b) She's *extremely* happy.
(14a) She spoke *clearly*.
(14b) She spoke *very clearly*.

Modifiers of Adjectives

Very is a very common adverb that can modify an adjective. Some other examples are: *amazingly* peaceful, *awfully* sorry, *deeply* concerned, *extremely* cold, *perfectly* all right, *strikingly* tall, *terribly* sorry, *fairly* small, *nearly* complete, *pretty* good, *rather* late, *relatively* big, *quite* normal.

Exercise 4 (intermediate)

Use an adverb before the adjective in the following sentences. Try to use different adverbs.

1. Pradip is tall.
2. The dress was expensive.

3. She was sorry.
4. She was concerned about your health.
5. Her husband is short-tempered.
6. That curve is dangerous.
7. We should leave as it is dark outside.
8. It is normal for us to work till eight in the evening.
9. It is a rare monument.
10. This room is small.

Intensifiers: *very, too* and *very much*

- We use *very* before an adjective or an adverb, when we mean *to a high degree.*

  (15) It is *very* hot in the month of May. (very + adjective)
  (16) She ran *very* fast. (very + adverb)

- By contrast, *too* implies excess and means *more than the desirable.*

  (17) That shirt is *too* bright.
  (18) It is *too* hot to go out.
  (19) He works *too* slowly to finish the office work by 5 o'clock.

- We use *very much* before some verbs to emphasise how we feel about things.

  (20) We *very much* appreciate your concern.

Exercise 5 (advanced)

Fill in the blanks with *very, too,* or *very much*.

1. Her brother is .... tall.
2. We enjoyed the play ....
3. She didn't think that her assistant was .... humorous.
4. It is .... hot and I can't drink it.
5. I .... agree with your plan.
6. She was .... engrossed in watching the TV to have noticed your presence.
7. The coat looks .... heavy.
8. She seems .... upset. She regrets losing her temper at the party.
9. You can ring him up but I .... doubt that he'll be in his office.
10. This room is .... small for anyone to work.
11. Her mother is not .... happy with her behaviour.

12. They played .... well in the first half.
13. She talked to me .... politely during the interval.
14. Although I .... want to attend the meeting, I can't because I have a toothache.
15. These shoes are .... big for me to wear with this dress.
16. I .... appreciate this opportunity to speak to you.
17. She is .... tall.
18. She is .... tall to wear this striped dress.
19. We .... enjoyed the concert.
20. She ran .... fast at the sports meet.

Unit 29

ADVERBS 3

Focus adverbs

Even and *only* are usually used in the mid position, but one can use them before the subject if one wanted to refer to the subject.

(1) *Only* I watched TV last night. (no one else watched TV last night)
(2) I *only* watched TV last night. (but didn't do anything else)
(3) *Even* she can play tennis. (one doesn't expect her to)
(4) She can *even* play tennis. (in addition to other sports)

Exercise 1 (intermediate)

Rewrite the following sentences twice using *even* or *only*. Use them in two positions, once in the beginning and once in the middle of the sentence.

1. My father can sing.
2. My brother passed the test.
3. Monica can speak German.
4. She can drive a car.
5. He can direct a film.

Negative adverbs and inversion

Some adverbs such as *hardly, little, never,* and *scarcely, rarely, seldom* have a negative effect.

(5) She has *hardly* any money. (very little money)
(6) I have *never* seen such a man.

When these adverbs are used in the beginning of a sentence, there is inversion of the helping verb and the subject as in the case of a yes/no question.

(7) *Hardly has she* got any money.
(8) *Never have I* seen such a man.

Exercise 2 (Advanced)

Rewrite the following sentences. Use the underlined negative adverbs in the beginning.

1. I seldom go to Mumbai.
2. Rakesh little realises that it is very important.
3. I've never done such a thing in my life.
4. I'll never visit her house again.
5. She can barely lift this box.

Unit 30

MODAL VERBS 1

General characteristics of modal verbs

Modal verbs are also called modal auxiliaries. The purpose for which they are used is different from that of other auxiliaries or helping verbs and so they are treated separately. The following are the modal verbs used in English:

can, could, may, might, will, would, shall, should and *must*

These modal verbs are also referred to as *central modals,* since there are other verbs which function as modals. They are called *marginal modals.* Marginal modals are *dare, need, ought to* and *used to.*

Both central and marginal modals are used primarily to express our relationship with other people. These are used to indicate our attitude towards what we are saying.

Special characteristics of modal verbs

- A modal is always followed by the base form of the verb.

  (1) Prema *can sleep* on the floor.
  (2) She *might visit* you in the evening.

- Negatives can be formed by adding *not* after the modal, or by adding *n't* to the modal. In the case of *ought to,* the negative particle *not* is used after *ought.*

  (3) *I may not come* tomorrow.
  (4) She *couldn't attend* classes regularly.
  (5) Sagar *ought not to have done* this.

- Questions are formed by placing the modal in front of the subject. In the case of *ought to, ought* is placed before the subject and *to* is placed after the subject.

  (6) *Could you give* me a call in the evening?
  (7) *Ought we to* go now?

Exercise 1 (elementary)

Rewrite the following sentences as their negative forms.

1. We will play football this evening.
   We will not (won't) play football this evening.
2. Fyaz can write interesting essays.
3. They may visit us tomorrow.
4. She could finish her work in time.
5. You should write to him.
6. You must sit there.
7. They should visit the hostel.
8. Renu will attend the class on Monday.
9. Vijay may take your car.
10. He can attend my lecture today.
11. It will rain in the evening.
12. You must phone her.
13. They ought to have done it.
14. She must write him a letter.
15. I could play football when I was a child.

Exercise 2 (elementary)

Change the following sentences into yes/no questions.

1. Professor Kumar will take our class tomorrow.
   Will Professor Kumar take our class tomorrow?
2. I could meet you at the bus stand.
3. He will go now.
4. I can eat this piece of bread.
5. We may leave this room now.
6. You can see me in the evening.
7. I may borrow your car.
8. You will open the window.
9. We shall watch the film.
10. We ought to wait for some more time.
11. She can go with you.
12. It will rain tomorrow.
13. I must do it now.
14. She can make some tea.
15. I may see your garden.

Unit 31

MODAL VERBS 2

ABILITY, PERMISSION, OFFERS AND INVITATIONS

ABILITY

We can use *can* to talk about someone's ability in the present.

(1) Sarita *can* work for twenty hours a day.
(2) Farida *can* drive a truck.

Notice that sentence (1) can be paraphrased as:

(3) Sarita is *able/has the ability* to drive a truck.

We can use *could* to express past ability, that is, the ability that one possessed in the past.

(4) Sonali *could* work for twenty hours when she was a girl.
(5) Ajay *could* play the guitar when he was in college.

Notice that sentence (4) can be paraphrased as:

(6) Sonali *was able to* play for twenty hours when she was a girl.

PERMISSION/ASKING FOR PERMISSION

The four modal verbs *can, could, may* and *might* can be used to ask for permission.
Can is quite common and is the most informal.

(7) *Can* I use your telephone, (please)?

Could is tentative and is used when there is a doubt that permission will be granted.

(8) *Could* I use your telephone, (please)?

May is more formal than *can* and *could* and is more respectful.

(9) *May* I use your telephone, (please)?

Might is the most polite but is rare and least common.

(10) *Might* I use your telephone, (please)?

All these sentences from (7) to (10) can be paraphrased as:

(11) *Am I* allowed to use your telephone?

We use two modals *can (not)* or *may (not)* to give or refuse permission in everyday situations.

(12) You *can/may* use the library.

The meaning of sentence (12) is that:

(13) You are permitted to use the library. *or*
You are allowed to use the library.

EXERCISE 1 (INTERMEDIATE)

Rewrite the following sentences using *can, could,* or *may* in place of the underlined words.

1. He is able to drive a car.
   He can drive a car.
2. Am I allowed to borrow your car? (tentative).
   Could I borrow your car?
3. You are not allowed/permitted to smoke here.
   You cannot smoke here or you may not smoke here.
4. Rita is able to fly a plane.
5. Am I allowed to drive this car? (informal)
6. Rehman was able to attend the meeting yesterday as he took the morning train to Jabalpur.
7. She is able to walk ten kilometres everyday.
8. You are allowed to go on leave next week.
9. Am I allowed to borrow some books from the library? (tentative)
10. They were able to operate this machine, when they were young.
11. Are we allowed to take part in the discussion? (tentative)
12. Are we allowed to attend the conference? (formal)
13. He is permitted to participate in the national games.
14. You are allowed to borrow my car tomorrow.
15. You are not allowed to park your car here.
16. Am I allowed to use your telephone? (informal)
17. You are not permitted to smoke here.
18. My grandfather was not able to swim.
19. You are not permitted to travel in the first AC compartment.
20. Am I allowed to use your pen? (tentative)

Offers and Invitations

For offering and inviting, we use the phrase *'Would you like .....?'*

(14) *Would you like* a cup of tea?

(15) *Would you like* to attend the lecture tomorrow?

Exercise 2 (advanced)

How do you offer the following to someone? Write sentences as shown in the example.

a cup of tea	an orange	a chapati
some juice	some vegetables	some potatoes
some milk	some dal	a mango

Would you like a cup of coffee?

Unit 32

MODAL VERBS 3

POSSIBILITY, REQUESTS AND SUGGESTIONS

POSSIBILITY

There are three modals – *may, might* and *could* – that can be used to express possibility.

(1) She *may be* at home now.
(2) She *might be* at home now.
(3) She *could be* at home now.

May indicates factual possibility but if we are less sure we may use *might* or *could.*

Sentences (1), (2) and (3) express possibility in the present. One could also express possibility in the future.

(4) Mrs Bhalla *might take* our class tomorrow.
(5) We *could go* out for a walk in the evening.

EXERCISE 1 (INTERMEDIATE)

Rewrite the following sentences using *may, might or could.*

1. It is possible that it will rain tomorrow. (factual possibility)
   It may rain tomorrow.
2. It is possible that he is attending the meeting. (less sure)
   He could/might be attending the meeting.
3. It is possible that I will win the prize. (less sure)
4. It is possible that the best of pilots make judgment errors. (factual possibility)
5. It is possible that Sunita is in her office. (factual possibility)
6. It is possible that the state will be placed under the Governor's rule. (less sure)
7. It is possible that Debashish will visit Ahmedabad next week. (factual possibility)
8. It is possible that Kailash is on his way to the bank. (less sure)
9. It is possible that the team is preparing for the final match. (factual possibility)
10. It is possible that our team will win the match. (less sure)

11. It is possible that the house is still vacant. (factual possibility)
12. It is possible that Rita will pass the examination. (factual possibility)
13. It is possible that they are married. (less sure)
14. It is possible that the engine will work. (factual possibility)
15. It is possible that they are listening. (less sure)

We can express the possibility of an event happening by using *be + present participle* form of the main verb with *may, might* or *could.*

(6) Vanita *may be working* at home.
(7) Shweta *might be studying* hard.

In order to express the past possibility, we can use *have + past participle* form along with *may, might* or *could.*

(8) She *may/might/could have been* home yesterday.
(9) Vanita *could have worked* at home yesterday.
(10) Shweta *might have studied* hard.
(11) Shweta *might have been studying* hard.

Exercise 2 (advanced)

Rewrite the following statements as 'possible' statements with the help of *may, might,* or *could.*

1. He is in his office now.
   He may/might/could be in his office now.
2. She watched TV yesterday.
   She/may/might/could have watched TV yesterday.
3. He was at home yesterday.
4. Anita will be at home tomorrow.
5. The plane left Amritsar in the morning.
6. The plane will leave Amritsar at 5 pm.
7. They will open school at 8 o'clock.
8. They opened school at 8 o'clock.
9. She was playing cards in the afternoon.
10. He was sleeping at 4 o'clock.
11. He will be working today.
12. She has left.
13. They have finished their work.
14. She is in the library.
15. They are working in the office.

Requests

We can use *can, could, may, might, will and would* to make requests.

- *Can* is used to make a simple request in an informal manner.

  (12) *Can* I *sit* with you?
  (13) *Can* I *have* some milk, please?

- *Could* is also used to make a request. The use of *could* is considered tentative and therefore more polite than *can*.

  (14) *Could* I *see* the Vice-chancellor, please?

- *May* and *might* are more formal than *can* and *could* to make requests. Requests made with *might* are very formal and are therefore rare and unusual.

  (15) *May* I *know* your name, please?
  (16) *Might* I *know* if the results have been declared? (rare)

- *Will* and *would* can also be used to make polite requests for actions in the immediate or distant future.

  (17) *Will/would* you *open* the door, please? (now)
  (18) *Will/would* you *lend* me your book? (now or later)

Suggestions

- The most common way to make a suggestion is by using an interrogative sentence beginning with *shall* and *we*.

  (19) *Shall* we *see* this film today?
  (20) *Shall* we *leave* now?

- Another way of making a suggestion is to use *could/might* in a declarative sentence.

  (21) We *could see* this film today.
  (22) You *might build* your house there.

Exercise 3 (intermediate)

Rewrite each of the following sentences as a request or a suggestion with the help of the modal verb suggested in brackets.

1. I want to read this book. (a request with *can*)
   Can I read this book?

2. I want to attend the French classes. (a request with *may*)
   May I attend the French classes?
3. We may attend the prayer. (a suggestion with *shall*)
   Shall we attend the prayer?
4. We may meet the Principal. (a suggestion with *could*)
   We could meet the Principal.
5. You may have lunch with us tomorrow. (a request with *would)*
6. You may switch on the television, please. (a request with *will*)
7. We may have dinner now. (a suggestion with *shall*)
8. I want to drink a glass of mango juice. (a request with *can*)
9. You lend me your car, please. (a request with *could*)
10. I want to meet the Principal. (a request with *could*)
11. I want to borrow this book from the library. (a request with *may*)
12. You may drop me at my hostel. (a request with *would*)
13. We walk down to the market. (a suggestion with *could*)
14. You may shut the window, please. (a request with *will)*
15. I want to discuss this issue with the director. (a request with *may*)
16. I want to have some potatoes. (a request with *can*)
17. You may switch on the fan, please. (a request with *would*)
18. I want to borrow your book. (a request with *could*)
19. We may start the meeting now. (a suggestion with *shall*)
20. You may go out for dinner tonight. (a suggestion with *shall)*
21. I want to drink some coke. (a request with *can)*
22. I want the salt, please. (a request with *could*)
23. You may switch on the TV, please. (a request with *will)*
24. You may show me that card. (a request with *would)*
25. We want to play cricket in the afternoon. (a request with *can)*

Unit 33

MODAL VERBS 4

NECESSITY AND OBLIGATION

NECESSITY AND COMPULSION

- We use *must* and *have to* to show that it is necessary to do something.

  (1) You *must/have to attend* the meeting tomorrow.

- Sometimes, there is a difference between *must* and *have to.* If the necessity/obligation comes from the speaker, the auxiliary *must* is used. If the obligation is from outside, then *have to* is used.

  (2) I haven't telephoned Mukesh for ages. I *must telephone* him today.

  (3) Please get her breakfast ready. She *has to reach* office by 10 o'clock.

- We use *must* to talk about the present and future. There is no past tense form of *must.* Therefore *had to* is used to express past obligation. *Must* also does not agree with third person singular subject whereas *have to* does.

  (4) We *must leave* now.
  (5) You *must attend* school tomorrow.
  (6) She *has to attend* the meeting.
  (7) She *had to attend* the meeting yesterday.

EXERCISE 1 (ADVANCED)

Fill in the blanks in the following sentences with either *must* or *have to.* Note that in some cases, it is possible to use either.

1. It is going to rain soon. I .... leave now.
2. Mary was not too well yesterday. She .... leave office early.
3. It was not a direct flight to London. They .... change the plane in Paris.
4. When you visit Lucknow next time, you .... stay with us.

5. I .... speak to him today, so that my leave is sanctioned before I leave Delhi.
6. You .... get your leave sanctioned before you leave for the USA.
7. My grandmother suddenly fell ill last night. We .... call the doctor.
8. It's getting late. We .... leave now.
9. I .... pay a higher fare to travel in AC 2nd class.

Obligation

When we want to introduce the meaning of obligation, that is, when we wish to say that something needs to be done or is the right thing to do, we use *ought to* or *should*.

(8) You *ought to exercise* during the camp.

(9) He *should report* to work at 9 am everyday.

The past tense of these two modal verbs are *ought to have* and *should have*.

(10) She *ought to have met* me at the airport yesterday.

Should and *ought to* can be used to express probability either in the present or in the future.

(11) Rita *should have/ought to have reached* Bilaspur by now.

(12) Venissa *should/ought to be* there soon.

Exercise 2 (advanced)

Rewrite the following sentences using *must, ought to, should, ought to have,* or *should have*.

1. It is necessary for you to submit the application today.
   You must submit the application today.
2. He was obliged to inform you that he should not meet you today.
   He should have/ought to have informed you that he would not meet you today.
3. It is necessary for you to meet the doctor next week.
4. Rekha is obliged to support her younger brothers.
5. It is necessary for her to use glasses.
6. We are obliged to respect our teachers.
7. They were obliged to see the Principal in the morning.

8. It is necessary to finish our work on time.
9. He was obliged to take your permission before he took a week's leave.
10. Visitors are obliged to park their vehicles outside the gate.
11. You are obliged to report to work within ten days.
12. It is necessary for students to wear their games uniform on Saturdays.
13. It is necessary that you stop smoking.
14. You are obliged to stop smoking here.
15. She is in the hospital. You are obliged to go and see her there.

Needn't and mustn't

Needn't expresses the sense of not having the necessity to do something.

(13) You *needn't take* the test. (You have already passed it.)
(14) Karim *needn't pay* the money. (Somebody has already paid for him.)

Mustn't is used when something should not be done.

(15) Since John has a cold, he *mustn't come* out in the rain. (If he does, the cold will worsen.)
(16) You *mustn't miss* this rare opportunity. (You are not likely to get it again.)

Exercise 3 (advanced)

Fill in the blanks with *needn't* or *mustn't*.

1. You .... go to the market. I've already bought vegetables for two days.
2. You .... go out to the market. Curfew has been clamped over the city.
3. Rekha .... neglect her studies. She didn't do well in the last test.
4. Vinita .... attend extra classes. She did very well in the last term.
5. I .... build a house. My father has transferred our ancestral house to me.
6. He suffers from high blood pressure. He .... eat a lot of salt.
7. You .... go to work today. It has been declared a public holiday.
8. You .... take leave today. There is a lot of work that needs to be finished.
9. The children .... disturb the neighbours.
10. You .... visit her in the hospital everyday. Her sister is constantly by her side.

Unit 34

COMPLEX SENTENCES

The simple sentences that we studied in units 1 and 2 comprise only one clause.

(1) That girl is very talented.
(2) The judge found the complaint false.

	S	Trv	Od	(Adv)
(3)	I	saw	him	then.
(4)	He	was coming		out of his office.

A sentence that consists of two or more clauses is a *complex sentence.*

Both sentences (3) and (4) are simple sentences. We can combine sentences (3) and (4) in such a way that sentence (4) is used as an adverbial in the position of *then* in sentence (3). We can form a complex sentence by combining sentences (3) and (4) as follows:

	S	Trv	Od	(Adv)
(5)	I	saw	him	while he was coming out of his office.

Notice that *while he was coming out of his office* is an adverbial clause. A complex sentence may have two or more subject–predicate structures. In other words a complex sentence comprises a main (principal) clause and one or more subordinate clauses. A subordinate clause functions as one of the elements of the main clause. For example, in sentence (5), *I saw him* is the main clause and *while he was coming out of his office* is the subordinate clause because it functions as the adverbial of the main clause.

A subordinate clause is attached to the main clause with the help of a *conjunction.* Notice that *while* is the conjunction used with the subordinate clause in sentence (5).

Now consider the following simple sentences.

	S	Trv	Od
(6)	I	know	it.
(7)	Mohan	is	a bank manager.

We can combine sentences (6) and (7) in such a way that sentence (7) is used in place of *Od* in sentence (6). The conjunction required to combine sentences (6) and (7) is *that.* So we get the following sentence:

	S	Trv	Od
(8)	I	know that	Mohan is a bank manager.

The clause *that Mohan is a bank manager* functions as the direct object of the main clause and is thus the subordinate clause. There is an easy test to identify the number of clauses in a sentence. We may count the number of main verbs in a sentence and the rule is that the number of main verbs in a sentence is equal to the number of clauses in a sentence (see unit 9 for main verbs).

(9) Meenakshi is *reading* a book.

Notice that sentence (9) has only one main verb, that is, *reading.* Therefore, it has only one clause and is a simple sentence. But consider the following:

(10) I *went* to his house because he *needed* my help.

Sentence (10) has two main verbs, *went* and *needed* and therefore, it is a complex sentence with two clauses. The subordinate clause is *because he needed my help.*

(11) I *feel* that he will *come* here if we *send* him the money.

Notice that sentence (11) has three clauses because it has three main verbs: *feel, come* and *send.* The subordinate clauses are: *that he will come here* and *if we send him the money.* The conjunctions used with the subordinate clauses are *that* and *if.*

Notice that a subordinate clause may also be used at the beginning of a sentence:

(12) *When I last met him,* he was writing a novel.
(13) *That the earth is round* is a fact.

When I last met him and *That the earth is round* are subordinate clauses. *When* and *that* are conjunctions in sentences (12) and (13) respectively.

Exercise 1 (Advanced)

Identify the main clause, the subordinate clause and the conjunction in each of the following sentences.

1. **He told me that the Prime Minister would visit Lucknow.**
   Main clause: He told me
   Subordinate clause: that the Prime Minister would visit Lucknow
   Conjunction: that
2. **I shall help you if you pass this examination.**
3. **He noticed that she was wearing his daughter's dress.**
4. **The fact is that he never attended the meeting.**
5. **That the building has collapsed is unbelievable.**
6. **I shall see you after I have finished the lecture.**
7. **Although I reached the college at 9 am, I couldn't see the Principal.**
8. **That she was coming was known to everybody.**
9. **The rumour was that she has been dismissed.**
10. **As Shakti had returned early, we went out for a walk.**
11. **We will go out when you are ready.**
12. **You may leave the class as soon as you have finished your paper.**
13. **I last met him when he lived in London.**
14. **I'll visit Delhi if you grant me leave.**
15. **That our team would win the match was expected by everyone.**

NOUN CLAUSES 1

A noun clause is a subordinate clause that can be used in one of the positions that are usually occupied by a noun/pronoun/noun phrase in a sentence – subject, object and complement.

'THAT' NOUN CLAUSE

A very frequent noun clause that we would need for oral and written communication is the *that-noun clause.* It is called a *that*-noun clause because the conjunction used before the noun clause is *that.*

A. Subject

A *that*-noun clause can function as the subject in a sentence.

(1) *That he will be elected the Prime Minister* is expected by everyone.

(2) *That she had seen this film* proves her interest in art films.

Notice that *That he will be elected the Prime Minister* and *That she had seen this film* are the subjects in sentences (1) and (2) respectively.

EXERCISE 1 (ELEMENTARY)

Combine sentences *a* and *b* in the following pairs of sentences in such a way that sentence *b* becomes the *that*-noun clause in the subject position of sentence *a*.

1. a. It did not come as a surprise to anyone.
   b. India won the one-day series.
   That India won the one-day series did not come as a surprise to anyone.
2. a. It has brought credit to the school.
   b. Kunal has stood first in the ISC examination.
3. a. It indicates her popularity in the international community.
   b. She will meet the President of the USA.

4. a. It has not changed our government's policy.
   b. The troops have been withdrawn.
5. a. It raised the morale of the battalion.
   b. Rajinder was promoted as Lieutenant Colonel.
6. a. It is a known fact.
   b. America is a superpower.
7. a. It is very creditable for us.
   b. India is the largest democracy.
8. a. It will help him in passing the examination.
   b. He can speak English well.
9. a. It has come as a surprise.
   b. She has become a pilot.
10. a. It was clear.
    b. He had made a mistake.

B. Direct object

A *that*-noun clause can function as the direct object of a monotransitive or ditransitive verb.

(3) I know *that Mohinder has passed the examination.*
(4) She assumed *that you would attend the meeting.*
(5) He told me *that she was not right.*

The italicised clauses have been used as direct objects in the above sentences. It is possible to drop *that* at the object position. *That* as a conjunction can be dropped in an informal situation. For example, we could say:

(6) I know *Mohinder has passed the examination.*
(7) He told me *she was not right.*

Some of the verbs that can have *that*-noun clause at the direct object position are:

accept	believe	feel	know
admit	declare	find	mention
agree	discover	hear	reply
announce	dream	hope	report
assume	explain	write	say

Exercise 2 (elementary)

Combine sentences *a* and *b* in the following pairs of sentences in such a way that sentence *b* becomes the *that*-noun clause in the direct object position of sentence *a*.

1. a) Kamlesh accepted it.
   b) Her sister had taken the book.
   Kamlesh accepted that her sister had taken the book.
2. a) She told me something.
   b) You were coming here on Tuesday.
3. a) I regret it.
   b) She did not give me the discount.
4. a) Vikram dreamt it.
   b) He had become a general.
5. a) We heard it.
   b) You are going to the USA.
6. a) Sunita knows it.
   b) Sridhar has passed the examination.
7. a) Ajay found it.
   b) His house had been occupied.
8. a) They said it.
   b) The taxes would not be increased.
9. a) She feels it.
   b) We should buy a car.
10. a) The officer announced it.
    b) There would be an increase in pay.

C. Subject complement

That-noun clauses can be used as subject complement after the linking verb *be.*

(8) The fact is *that he never attended the meeting.*
(9) The recommendation was *that all the employees should be promoted.*

There is a limited number of nouns that can have the *that*-noun clause in the subject complement position, after the linking verb. Some of these nouns are: *advice, answer, assumption, belief, decision, explanation, fact, feeling, hope, reply, remark, report* etc.

Exercise 3 (Elementary)

Combine sentences *a* and *b* in the following pairs of sentences in such a way that sentence *b* becomes the *that*-noun clause used as the complement of the subject of sentence *a*.

1. a. The chances are there.
   b. We'll win the match.

2. a. The suggestion was this.
   b. The meeting should be held after two months.
3. a. The assumption is this.
   b. Democracy will survive.
4. a. The decision was this.
   b. Varoon would be given a scholarship.
5. a. My advice is this.
   b. You should attend the interview tomorrow.
6. a. The answer is this.
   b. You can join duty.
7. a. The feeling is this.
   b. There should be no examination.
8. a. The news is this.
   b. India has won the cricket match.
9. a. The hope is this.
   b. We shall get the help.
10. a. The belief is this.
    b. Everyone is equal in democracy.

D. With 'it'

That-noun clauses can be used with *it* in the subject position. *It* is called the introductory subject and the *that*-noun clause is called the delayed subject.

(10) It is obvious *that she can't do it.*
(11) It is important *that you go to the station.*

Exercise 4 (elementary)

Combine the clauses under column A and column B to make as many appropriate sentences as possible.

A	B
It was sad	that someone entered our house.
It is clear	that she never attends the meeting.
It is obvious	that we have to do it.
It is true	that she couldn't attend the marriage.
It is good	that Karishma has passed the examination.

E. Adjective complement

The *that*-noun clause can sometimes be used as the complement of an adjective.

(12) I am glad *that she has passed.*

(13) We are annoyed *that you had not informed us.*

Some of the adjectives and past participles that can be followed by a *that*-clause are: *afraid, aware, alarmed, amazed, annoyed, astonished, certain, confident, disturbed, glad, grateful, happy, hopeful, pleased, proud, sad, shocked, sorry.* It is possible to drop the conjunction *that* in an informal style:

(14) I am glad *she has passed.*

Exercise 5 (elementary)

Combine the clauses under column A and column B to make as many appropriate sentences as possible.

A	B
I am disappointed	that Rahul could do it.
Mrinalini is certain	that she'll pay you the money.
She is astonished	that he'll win the prize.
I am hopeful	that she'll be selected.
He is confident	that the incident occurred.

Exercise 6 (intermediate)

Combine sentences *a* and *b* in the following pairs of sentences in such a way that sentence *b* is used as the *that*-noun clause at an appropriate position in sentence *a*.

1. a) It has surprised us.
   b) She has failed in the examination.
2. a) He believed it.
   b) She could do it.
3. a) She said something.
   b) She could look into the matter.
4. a) It is good.
   b) She has come.
5. a) He told me something.
   b) You were coming on Tuesday.
6. a) It was clear.
   b) He had made a mistake.
7. a) It is a fact.
   b) The earth is round.
8. a) He was certain.

b) You would attend the meeting.
9 a) I am confident.
b) I can do it.
10. a) I feel it.
b) He should be given a raise.
11. a) The Principal announced it.
b) The exams would begin on 2nd April.
12. a) The assumption is this.
b). The inflation rate will not increase.
13. a) The fact is this.
b) We have paid all the instalments.
14. a) I am sorry.
b) She behaved in such a manner.
15. a) It is true.
b) She wrote this letter.
16. a) It was appreciated by everyone.
b) Monica completed this work.
17. a) She knows it.
b) You'll attend the meeting.
18. a) Our advice was this.
b) They could start the degree in computer science.
19. a) She is glad.
b) You attended her sister's marriage.
20. a) I dreamt it.
b) I had stood first in the exam.
21. a) It enhanced the reputation of our company.
b) He has been awarded Padma Bhushan.
22. a) I am hopeful.
b) We'll get the aid.
23. a) It is important.
b) You attend the meeting.
24. a) She assumed it.
b) You would attend the meeting.
25. a) The decision was this.
b) She would be promoted.

EXERCISE 7 (ADVANCED)

Fill in the blanks with an appropriate *that-noun clause.*

1. I thought ....
I thought that you were coming tomorrow.

2. It is good ....
   It is good that she has been promoted.
3. .... is a fact.
4. The fact is ....
5. She knew ....
6. It is believed ....
7. Rakesh told me ....
8. She knows ....
9. It is clear ....
10. I am happy ....
11. .... has made everyone happy.
12. I agree ....
13. She has written ....
14. The assumption is ....
15. The report is ....
16. .... was not a surprise for anyone.
17. She dreamt ....
18. We hoped ....
19. It is important ....
20. I am astonished ....
21. The teacher announced ....
22. We assumed ....
23. .... has not affected our policy.
24. They found ....
25. My feeling is ....

EXERCISE 8 (ADVANCED)

Identify and write down the main clause, the *that*-noun clause and the function of the noun clause in the following sentences. In some sentences *that* has been dropped.

1. That she had become a pilot has thrilled everyone.
   main clause: .... has thrilled everyone.
   that-noun clause: That she had become a pilot (used at the subject position)
2. The Minister announced that the bridge would be constructed within a week.
   main clause: The Minister announced ....
   that-noun clause: that the bridge would be constructed within a week. (used as the direct object)
3. She feels that we should buy a vehicle.

4. That India is the largest democracy is very creditable.
5. The feeling is that there should be no examination.
6. The hope is that we shall get help.
7. Kiran is certain that she will get this job.
8. I am afraid you cannot join this course.
9. It is clear that he is not going to help you.
10. That his father is alive is no less than a miracle.
11. She is insisting that we should pay an advance on the rent.
12. Mohini suggested that we should go on a vacation.
13. She is astonished that Rahul could do it.
14. I am convinced that he is a great writer.
15. I am glad that she has come.
16. The reply is that we should start the project.
17. The report is that the interest rate has decreased.
18. We were hopeful that she would survive.
19. It is possible that she has reached Delhi.
20. The general has ordered that the troops should move immediately.
21. She assumed you would attend the meeting.
22. That she does not know him demonstrates her lack of social skills.
23. He told me she was not right.
24. The news is that India has won the cricket match.
25. We are sorry that we could not call you back.

Unit 36

NOUN CLAUSES 2

Noun Clauses Derived from Questions

In Unit 35, we discussed that *that-noun clauses* can be derived from statements. In this unit, we shall discuss some of the important noun clauses that are derived from questions.

A. Wh-clauses

(1) Where has she left the keys?

This is a wh-question. We can use it as a subordinate clause in a sentence such as:

(2) I don't know *where she has left the keys.*

You will notice that *the wh-clause* (which is derived from a wh-question) has the structure of a statement, that is, there is no auxiliary inversion. Secondly, the wh-word itself functions as a conjunction.

(3) She asked me *why they were not coming.*

Exercise 1 (intermediate)

Combine sentences *a* and *b* in the following pairs of sentences in such a way that sentence *b* is used in the object position in sentence *a*. Change the word order of the wh-question to that of the wh-clause.

1. a. I never believed it.
   b. What did you tell me?
   I never believed what you told me.
2. a. She didn't know it.
   b. How would Nasreen respond to her question?
3. a. I know it.
   b. When did she meet him?
4. a. Can you remember it?
   b. Where have you parked your scooter?
5. a. Tell me this.
   b. How will you manage?
6. a. I don't know anything.

b. Why didn't she attend the party?

7. a. Mary asked me something.
   b. What time would the train arrive?
8. a. I can't tell it.
   b. Why did she arrive late?
9. a. I know it.
   b. Why didn't he take the examination?
10. a. I'd like to know it.
    b. What does he want?

Exercise 2 (Intermediate)

Complete the following sentences with the wh-noun clauses.

1. Where is the bank?
   Can you tell me <u>where the bank is?</u>
2. What time will the plane arrive?
   Do you know .... ?
3. Who was Akbar's father? Tell me ....
4. When can I leave office? May I know .... ?
5. When did you meet her? I would like to know ....
6. How much does it cost? She knows ....
7. Who's knocking at the door? I wonder ....
8. Where does Randhir live? Do you know .... ?
9. What does he want? I want to know ....
10. What time did she leave? Do you remember .... ?

B. Yes-no question clauses

(4) Would Rita attend the party?

This is a yes-no question. We can use it as a subordinate clause in the object position in a sentence such as:

(5) She asked me *(whether/if) Rita would attend the party.*

Again the *yes-no question clause* (which is derived from the yes-no question) has the structure of a statement. The conjunction used is *whether* or *if.*

(6) I wonder *if he would take the examination.*

Exercise 3 (Intermediate)

Combine sentences *a* and *b* in the following pairs of sentences so that sentence *b* is used in the direct object position in sentence *a*.

1. a. I don't know anything.
   b. Was he present?
   I don't know if he was present.
2. a. She asked me something.
   b. Could Meena stay with them?
3. a. Jivan asked her something.
   b. Had she worked earlier?
4. a. I don't know anything.
   b. Is she attending the meeting?
5. a. She asked me something.
   b. Could you drive a car?
6. a. I want to know it.
   b. Should we ring her up?
7. a. Tell me this.
   b. Has she finished her lecture?
8. a. Do you know this?
   b. Did she go out alone?
9. a. She wants to know this.
   b. Do you have a spare pen?
10. a. I don't know anything.
    b. Is she coming to the meeting?

EXERCISE 4 (INTERMEDIATE)

Complete the following sentences with a yes-no question clause.

1. Did Rita work in that office?
   She asked me if Rita worked in that office.
2. Will she attend the meeting? I wonder ....
3. Is he ready? Ask him ....
4. Had Hari joined the company? Rani enquired ....
5. Has he played tennis today? I don't know ....
6. Has he finished the book? May I know ....
7. Could he come for dinner? She asked him ....
8. Did she know Rakesh? I asked her ....
9. Can you meet me tomorrow? I want to know ....
10. Could you help me? I wonder ....

EXERCISE 5 (ADVANCED)

Write down the main clause and the subordinate clause in the following sentences. Identify the type of subordinate clause.

1. He asked me why I couldn't attend the party.
   main clause: He asked me ....
   subordinate clause: why I couldn't attend the party. (wh-clause)
2. I wonder if she will meet you tomorrow.
3. I don't know when she will come.
4. Could you tell me where I can post this letter?
5. I wonder if he could lift that stone.
6. Mona enquired whether the postman had come.
7. Elizabeth asked me when the meeting would end.
8. I never believed what you told me.
9. She asked me if I could lend her my car.
10. Do you know how much it will cost?

Unit 37

RELATIVE CLAUSES 1

Relative clauses (also called adjectival clauses) are used after a noun or a noun phrase. They are always introduced by relative pronouns:

who	where
whom	when
which	why
whose	that

(1) The man *who is standing under the tree* is a policeman.
(2) The book *that you gave me last week* is very interesting.
(3) The boy *whose mother met you in school* wants to meet you.

A. The use of who

We use *who* in a relative clause when we are talking about *people.* We use *who* instead of *he/she/they. Who* is the subject of the relative clause.

(4a) A gentleman has left a note for you.
(4b) He came in the morning.
(4c) The gentleman (*he came in the morning*) left a note for you.
(4d) The gentleman (*who came in the morning*) left a note for you.
(5a) I met a coach.
(5b) He trained you.
(5c) I met the coach (*he trained you*).
(5d) I met the coach (*who trained you*).

Exercise 1 (Intermediate)

Combine the following pairs of sentences in such a way that sentence *b* of each pair is changed into the relative clause of sentence *a*.

1. a. The doctor wants to meet you.
   b. He has his clinic in your building.
   The doctor who has his clinic in your building wants to meet you.

2. a. I work with a boy.
   b. He is sitting with Rahul.
3. a. The lady is Meenakshi's mother.
   b. She works in our library.
4. a. The boy is my neighbour.
   b. He has stood first in school.
5. a. I am waiting for a girl.
   b. She joined our school yesterday.
6. a. This is the girl.
   b. She has been looking for you.
7. a. The director has been selected for the National Award.
   b. He made this film.
8. a She is the girl.
   b. She coaches our team.
9. a. The man is our Director.
   b. He was waving at Anuradha.
10. a. The boy asks a lot of questions.
    b. He is sitting in the front row.

B. The use of whom/who

Whom may be used as the object of the relative clause. However, nowadays *who* can also be used as the object of the relative clause. The difference between the use of *whom* and *who* as the object of the relative clause is that *whom* is used in a formal context and *who* is used in an informal context.

(6a) A girl has drafted this letter.
(6b) You selected her.
(6c) The girl (*you selected her*) has drafted this letter.
(6d) The girl (*who[m] you selected*) has drafted this letter.
(6e) The girl (*you selected*) has drafted this letter.

You can drop *whom/who* when it refers to the object position in the relative clause, as seen in sentence (6e).
You can also use *whom* with a preposition (*to/from/with whom* etc.).

(7) The boy (*with whom I shared the room*) has become my best friend.
(8) She is the girl (*for whom I bought these books*).

EXERCISE 2 (INTERMEDIATE)

Combine the following pairs of sentences. Change sentence *b* into a relative clause.

1. a. A girl was sitting in the chair.
   b. I had gone to meet her.
   The girl whom/who I had gone to meet was sitting in the chair.
2. a. The workers have arrived.
   b. You wanted to meet them.
3. a. The doctor is available today.
   b. You wanted to consult him.
4. a. A man gave an interview on TV this morning.
   b. I was talking about him.
5. a. The boy is my neighbour.
   b. You teach him at home.
6. a. My partner has left for the USA.
   b. I started my business with him.
7. a. The boy is very thin.
   b. She is going to be married to him.
8. a. These are the girls.
   b. You wanted to meet them.
9. a. The man had two grown-up daughters.
   b. We stayed with him.
10. a. I have selected a boy.
    b. You had recommended him.

C. The use of which/that

Which/that is used as a relative pronoun for non-human nouns such as *dog, cow, table, chair, book,* etc. *Which/that* can be used as either the subject or object of a relative clause. However, we use only *which* as the object of preposition in a relative clause.

(9) The scooter (*which/that is lying in the shed*) has been painted recently.

(10) The carriage (*by which we travelled*) had attractive windows.

EXERCISE 3 (INTERMEDIATE)

Combine the following pairs of sentences. Change sentence *b* into a relative clause.

1. a. Mohini works for a company.

b. It makes pens.

2. a. The car needs painting.
   b. Rakesh bought it last year.
3. a. She owns a house.
   b. It was constructed in the nineteenth century.
4. a. The dog is very fierce.
   b. It is chained to the door.
5. a. The story appeared in this newspaper.
   b. I was talking about this story.
6. a. We live in an area.
   b. It is threatened by floods every year.
7. a. I know the electronics shop.
   b. You want to visit it.
8. a. I bought the sofa set.
   b. My wife liked it.
9. a. The cat has run away.
   b. I brought it from Shillong.
10. a. He liked the house.
    b. You wanted to sell it.

D. The use of whose

Whose is a relative pronoun that is used to indicate possession.

(11a) The lady (*you bought her car*) is on the phone.
(11b) The lady (*whose car you bought*) is on the phone.

Exercise 4 (intermediate)

Combine the following pairs of sentences changing sentence *b* into a relative clause.

1. a. The man wants to meet you.
   b. His daughter is your secretary.
2. a. The necklace is very costly.
   b. You gave me the necklace.
3. a. The inspector has been transferred.
   b. You complained to him.
4. a. He knows the person.
   b. We have appointed him as our manager.
5. a. The television set is very good.
   b. We purchased it last year.
6. a. This is the man.
   b. His son is our college captain.

7. a. I've bought the book.
   b. You recommended it to me.
8. a. The girl is standing outside your office.
   b. Her father gave you this bag.
9. a. This is the dog.
   b. Its owner has disappeared.
10. a. The lion is very ferocious.
    b. It is roaring.
11. a. The doctor is on leave today.
    b. He saw you yesterday.
12. a. The taxi had very comfortable seats.
    b. We travelled to Kanpur by it.
13. a. The postman knows me.
    b. You gave my letter to him.
14. a. The people were late.
    b. We were waiting for them.
15. a. The people are nice.
    b. We are staying with them.
16. a. This is the table.
    b. I want to buy it.
17. a. The man is a doctor.
    b. I'm purchasing his house.
18. a. I'm quite annoyed with the boy.
    b. He talks too much in the class.
19. a. The young lady works for the *Times of India*.
    b. She wants to interview you.
20. a. The officer wants to take us to lunch.
    b. His son has joined IIM, Kolkata.

RELATIVE CLAUSES 2

Use of when, where and why

- *When* can be used in a relative clause when the clause is preceded by a noun referring to time, or a period of time, such as *year, day,* and *week.*

  (1) She remembers the day *when we first met.*

  a. She remembers the day.

  b. We first met *then/on that day.*

  c. She remembers the day (*we first met then/on that day*).

  d. She remembers the day (*when we first met*).

- *Where* is preceded by a noun referring to a place.

  (2) This is the house (*where I was born*).

  (3) I recently visited the town (*where I was born*).

- *Why* is used after the noun *reason.*

  (4) This is the reason (*why he didn't attend the meeting*).

Exercise 1 (elementary)

Fill in the blanks with *when, where* or *why.*

1. The year .... we got independence was a year of great expectations.
2. The reason .... I'm writing to you is to inform you of the change in schedule.
3. Do you remember the day .... we opened this shop?
4. I know the place .... she has kept the keys.
5. The reason .... they don't have their own house is that they've purchased an expensive car.
6. The decade .... the economic boom took place was a period of great prosperity.
7. I went to the room .... the old coins were found.
8. The year .... the World War II ended was a year of great political changes.
9. Do you remember the hotel .... we stayed last time?
10. She telephoned me to tell me the time .... we could meet.

EXERCISE 2 (INTERMEDIATE)

Combine the following pairs of sentences. Change sentence *b* into a relative clause.

1. a. I know a place.
   b. You can get excellent food there.
2. a. This is the time.
   b. We can start our new business now.
3. a. That is the house.
   b. I was born there.
4. a. The reason was I did not remember your address.
   b. I could not visit you for this reason.
5. a. There is a store in the corner.
   b. You can buy apple juice there.
6. a. This is the shop.
   b. You can get good suits there.
7. a. 1950 was the year.
   b. India became a Republic then.
8. a. The bank also deals with foreign exchange.
   b. I work there.
9. a. Do you remember the day?
   b. We went to school then.
10. a. The office is at the corner of the street.
    b. My wife works there.

Restrictive and non-restrictive relative clauses

The sentences given in Unit 37 and Unit 38 above are examples of restrictive relative clauses. A restrictive or defining clause is used to identify a noun.

(5) The man *who is drinking coffee* is an army officer.

(6) The films *that Doordarshan telecasts* are good entertainment.

In sentences (5) and (6), the relative clauses tell us which person or thing the speaker is referring to. The relative clause *who is drinking coffee* identifies or restricts the noun head *the man*. The relative clauses in sentences (5) and (6) answer the questions *which man* and *which films* respectively. A non-restrictive or non-defining relative clause, on the other hand, is used to give additional information about the noun.

(7) Dr Singh, *who is sitting in the library,* wants to see you.

(8) I met Sarada, *who had also come for the dinner.*

In sentences (7) and (8), the relative clauses do not tell us which person or thing the speaker means. We already know *Dr Singh* and *Sarada.* Usually a comma (,) is used at the beginning and another at the end of the non-restrictive relative clause when the non-restrictive relative clause comes in the middle of the main clause. When the relative clause comes at the end of the sentence, we put a comma only before the clause. We can also use *whose, whom, which* and *where* in non-restrictive relative clauses.

(9) Meenakshi, *whose mother teaches us English,* studies in my college.

(10) Mrs Soni has gone to England, *where her son has been living for five years.*

EXERCISE 3 (ADVANCED)

Combine the following pairs of sentences in such a way that sentence *b* is changed to a non-restrictive relative clause.

1. a. My sister is a pilot.
   b. She lives in Delhi.
   My sister, who lives in Delhi, is a pilot.
2. a. We stayed at the Taj Hotel.
   b. It is a beautiful building.
   We stayed at the Taj Hotel, which is a beautiful building.
3. a. I went to see Professor Nigam.
   b. He lives in Nehru Enclave.
4. a. Munira works for an electronic company.
   b. This company makes TV sets.
5. a. Our driver was late today.
   b. He is usually on time.
6. a. The girl over there is in our hockey team.
   b. I don't remember her name. (use *whose*)
7. a. The new college building will be opened next week.
   b. It has fifteen big halls.
8. a. Next month I'm visiting Mumbai.
   b. My brother lives there. (use *where*)
9. a. I often go to the stadium.
   b. It is only two miles from my house.
10. a. Mr Sharma has gone to office on scooter today.
    b. His car broke down in the morning. (use *whose*)

11. a. Rakesh was with me in the law school.
    b. His mother is your college doctor. (use *whose*)
12. a. I went to see the General Manager.
    b. He asked me to go to Chandigarh.
13. a. She introduced me to her youngest son.
    b. He is a captain in the army.
14. a. Our college principal has been nominated for the President's medal.
    b. He has written four books on English grammar.
15. a. Veena told me her telephone number.
    b. I wrote it down in my notebook.

Unit 39

ADVERBIAL CLAUSES 1

Adverbial clauses are also subordinate clauses. As in the case of other subordinate clauses, we need to use a conjunction before adverbial clauses.

(1) *When I reached his house*, he was writing a letter.
(2) I gave him money *because he was stranded.*

Position of adverbial clauses

The usual position of an adverbial clause in a sentence is right after the main clause.

(3) I reached the station *before the train left.*

An adverbial clause can also be placed before the main clause as in

(4) *When she reached office*, she didn't find anyone.

Sometimes, we can use an adverbial clause in the middle of the main clause.

(5) My uncle, *when he was young*, was a bank officer.

Adverbial clauses of time

Adverbial clauses of time are used to refer to a period of time or to a point of time with reference to another event. The conjunctions that can be used to introduce an adverbial clause of time are: *when, before, after, since, while, as* and *until.*

(6) I met Renu after *I had finished my work.*
(7) I have not seen him *since I left Amritsar.*
(8) *When I first saw him*, I thought he was a lawyer.

EXERCISE 1 (INTERMEDIATE)

Combine the sentences in the following pairs in such a way that sentence *b* of each pair is changed into an adverbial clause of time. Use one of the conjunctions given below. Note that more than one answer is possible in some cases.

while, as soon as, as, when, before, after, till

1. a. I was standing near the door ....
   b. I saw your car.
   I was standing near the door when I saw your car.
2. a. Please ring me up ....
   b. You reach the station.
3. a. .... , he went to see a movie.
   b. He had his lunch.
4. a. Usha looked very tired ....
   b. I met her last time.
5. a. .... , Vikram was watching TV.
   b. I was reading the newspaper.
6. a. .... , I visited all the leading educationists.
   b. I was in Delhi.
7. a. .... , his son was only two years old.
   b. Mr Agnihotri died.
8. a. They'll go home ....
   b. They've finished this project.
9. a. We'll visit India ....
   b. We've taken our exams.
10. a. .... , he went to bed.
    b. He had his dinner.
11. a. Wait here ....
    b. I return.
12. a. .... , you'll immediately be appointed manager.
    b. You pass your MBA.
13. a. We should do shopping ....
    b. The rain starts.
14. a. .... , I thought he was an army officer.
    b. I first saw him.
15. a. I haven't seen Ali ....
    b. He came back from the USA.

Adverbial clauses of reason

Adverbial clauses of reason are used to indicate the reason for the action in the main clause. The conjunctions generally used for clauses of reason are: *because, as* and *since.*

(9) I could not meet you, *because you were very busy.*

(10) *As he was the airport manager,* he had to listen to the passenger's complaint.

When an adverbial clause of reason is used in the beginning of the main clause, the usual conjunction used is either *as* or *since*.

Exercise 2 (intermediate)

Rewrite the sentence *b* in the following pairs as the adverbial clause of reason in the space given. Use *because, since* or *as*.

1. a. She wants to marry him, ...
   b. She likes him.
   She wants to marry him because she likes him.
2. a. ...., he should introduce the team to the chief guest.
   b. Rajesh is the captain.
3. a. Mukesh couldn't go out ....
   b. It was raining.
4. a. .... , I kept quiet.
   b. I knew my temper.
5. a. .... , I couldn't board the train.
   b. I was late.
6. a. You must sleep early tonight ....
   b. You have to get up early tomorrow morning.
7. a. .... , I asked for the payment of money.
   b. I had completed the work.
8. a. You should telephone Seema ....
   b. She needs your help.
9. a. I went to his office ....
   b. He wanted to meet me.
10. a. She has to help her parents.
    b. Farida is the eldest.

Adverbial clauses of manner

Adverbial clauses of manner are used to talk about someone's behaviour or the way something is done. Conjunctions that are usually used with clauses of manner are *as, as if, as though*..

(11) She behaves *as if she were the boss.*
(12) His face looked *as if it had been painted.*

In formal English, we use *were* instead of *was* in clauses of manner beginning with *as if* or *as though*. In informal English we may use *was* after the third person singular subject.

Exercise 3 (intermediate)

Combine the clauses in column A to the appropriate clause of manner in column B to make meaningful sentences.

A	B
1. She behaves	as though she had not slept for days.
2. I felt	as if he were a tennis player.
3. Mukesh talks	as if he were in love with her.
4. She looked	as if he had been a great singer
5. Rehman hits the ball	as though she had been a dancer.
6. Amitabh looked at Meenakshi	as though he were a politician.
7. Monica danced	as if she were a queen.
8. John sang	as if she had a fever.
9. She felt	as though she had come to a party.
10. Her dress made her look	as if I was going to faint.

Adverbial clauses of purpose

Adverbial clauses of purpose are used to indicate the purpose of an action. The most common conjunctions used to introduce clauses of purpose are *to, in order to*, and *so that*.

(13) My father gave me a piece of land *to build a house.*
(14) I worked hard *in order to pass the examination.*
(15) He took the car with him *so that his son would not drive it.*

Notice that the infinitive or (the first form of the verb) is used after *to* or *in order to. In order to* is more formal than *to.* A finite clause is used after *so that.* We often use *can, could, will, would* or *needn't* after *so that.*

Exercise 4 (intermediate)

Combine the clauses in column A with the clauses in column B to make meaningful sentences.

A	B
1. They built a garage	to meet the inspector.
2. The University has raised the fees	to find out about my result.

3. I studied hard	in order to improve your handwriting.
4. He took the umbrella	to catch the first train to Chennai.
5. The policeman went by car	to pay higher salaries to Professors.
6. Harsharan reached the railway station at 5 am	to pray.
7. They have gone to the temple	to gain experience in art films.
8. Write two pages everyday	so that they could park their car in it.
9. I rang up the school	so that he might not get wet.
10. She acted in my new film	in order to get a good grade.

EXERCISE 5 (ADVANCED)

Use the words/phrases given in brackets to construct adverbials of purpose. Combine them with the sentences given to make complex sentences.

1. a. I've taken leave.
   b. (a book on English grammar)
   I have taken leave so that I can write a book on English grammar.
2. a. Ramesh has gone to Delhi.
   b. (visa to Australia)
3. a. Gayatri left last night.
   b. (late night flight to Kolkata)
4. a. I met the Principal in the morning.
   b. (discussion the new English syllabus)
5. a. He visited the General Manager.
   b. (a new telephone connection)
6. a. I gave her my car.
   b. (Kanpur)
7. a. Rupali drove the car fast.
   b. (Vijayawada in time)
8. a. He went to the police station.
   b. (a complaint, his neighbour)
9. a. Sudha went to the public telephone booth in the evening.
   b. (her uncle, in Delhi)
10. a. I bought this shop.
    b. (a provision store)

EXERCISE 6 (ADVANCED)

Combine each of the following pairs of sentences into one sentence using the conjunction *so that*. Use *can, could, will* or *would* after *so that*.

1. a. Mrs Dhillon bought this house.
   b. She wanted to open a school.
   Mrs Dhillon bought this house so that she could open a school.
2. a. The General Manager went to Delhi by the afternoon flight.
   b. He wanted to see the Chairman in the evening.
3. a. Mr Sharma built a strong iron gate.
   b. He wanted his dog to remain inside the building.
4. a. I have cooked food.
   b. You can eat it at lunch.
5. a. He worked very hard.
   b. He wanted to finish the work by Monday.
6. a. I've opened the tap.
   b. You can fill water for the day.
7. a. They keep the windows open at night.
   b. They want to get fresh air.
8. a. Radhika has gone on long leave.
   b. She wants to finish her Ph.D.
9. a. I've given him the key to my house.
   b. He can stay there tonight.
10. a. The office order is typed in English and Hindi.
    b. All the employees can understand it.

EXERCISE 7 (ADVANCED)

Rewrite the following sentences. Use the correct tense and form of the verbs in brackets.

1. I read this novel while I (travel) to Srinagar.
2. I met him after the meeting (be) over.
3. Rajan (not meet) you until you have apologised to him.
4. She (be) very angry when she saw her son.
5. Please ring us up as soon as you (reach) Chennai.
6. I read this book when I (be) in class nine.
7. After I (reach) the airport, I found that I had left the ticket at home.
8. We reached home before our parents (return).
9. I saw him while he (cross) the road.
10. She (not write) since she went away.
11. John has not visited me since he (become) a doctor.

12. When I last saw him, he (live) in London.
13. He found this book while ne (come) to school.
14. When you've finished reading, I (serve) you dinner.
15. I saw him while he (come) out of school.

Exercise 8 (advanced)

Rewrite the following sentences. Choose the correct tense and form of the verbs in brackets.

1. Arvind is muscular because he (exercise) in the morning.
2. They (wear) light clothes because it was very hot outside.
3. As she (be) the eldest, she has to look after her younger sisters.
4. I took my son to Chennai, because he (pass) the IIT entrance examination.
5. As my father has gone go Delhi, I (go) to school alone.
6. I (drive) the car fast because I had to catch the train.
7. The flowers have got natural colour, because they (use) natural fertiliser.
8. Since it (rain), we couldn't play football yesterday.
9. I want to see this film, because it (be) a classic.
10. As he (never speak) to me, I didn't know when he was leaving.

Exercise 9 (advanced)

Write the following sentences. Choose the correct tense and form of the verbs in brackets.

1. She behaves as though she (be) an actress.
2. His dress made him look as if he (be) a cricket player.
3. Monica holds her head in her hands as though she (suffer) from an acute headache.
4. Ashok talked to us as if he (be) our director.
5. He treats her as if she (be) his junior.
6. She spoke to him as though she (be) a journalist.
7. Ali behaved as if he (not understand) the lecture.
8. I felt as if I (have) high fever.
9. His hair looked as if he (never take) a bath.
10. She looked as though she (be) angry with him.

Unit 40

ADVERBIAL CLAUSES 2

Conditional clauses

A conditional clause may indicate an open, hypothetical or an unfulfilled condition.

A. Open condition: An open condition is a real condition and can be fulfilled.

(1) *If I go to Mumbai,* I'll speak to your cousin.
(2) *If it is hot in the morning,* I won't go out.

Exercise 1 (intermediate)

Rewrite the following sentences. Use the correct tense and form of the verbs in brackets.

1. If I (go) to college, I'll speak to the Principal.
2. If Sonia takes up this job, she (be paid) well.
3. If you (heat) water under pressure, it changes into steam.
4. You (become) a good swimmer, if you swim everyday.
5. We (go) to sleep, if we're tired.
6. If you (want) to join this course, you must start preparing for the entrance test now.
7. If the college is open tomorrow, I (attend) Professor Chatterjee's lecture.
8. I (take) Monisha to Kanpur, if she visits Lucknow.
9. If I (have) time, I will buy a book.
10. You can get this book, if you (go) to the library.

B. Hypothetical condition: A conditional clause may contain a hypothetical condition, which cannot be fulfilled. Such clauses are used about situations we know do not exist.

(3) If he behaved well, I would help him.
(4) If she worked hard, she'd pass.
(5) If I were rich, I'd buy a bungalow.

Exercise 2 (intermediate)

Rewrite the following sentences. Use the correct tense and form of the verbs in brackets.

1. I (give) you money, if I had it; but I don't have any money.
2. If I (were) the Chief Minister, I (make) you the Home Minister.
3. I wouldn't mind going to Srinagar, if the company (give) me the time.
4. If I (knew) German, I (read) this book.
5. If I were you, I (not go) there.
6. If she (get up) early, she could catch the morning bus.
7. If he stopped smoking, he (be) much healthier.
8. If she (have) a guest room, we'd visit her, but she lives in a one-room flat.
9. If she passed the NET exam, she (get) a lecturer's position.
10. If he (work) hard, he'd pass.
11. If I met him, I (tell) him the truth.
12. If I had some money in the bank, I (invest) it in business.
13. If I (be) a doctor, I'd work in a village.
14. If I were you, I (not do) it.
15. If I (know) her address, I would tell you.

C. Unfulfilled condition in the past: The conditional clause contains a condition, which was not fulfilled in the past.

(6) *If he had written to me,* I would have arranged a taxi for him.

(7) *If we had taken our raincoats,* we would have not got wet.

It is possible to drop *if* in sentences (6) and (7) and use *had* before the subject.

(8) *Had he written to me,* I would have arranged a taxi for him.

(9) *Had we taken our raincoats,* we would not have got wet.

EXERCISE 3 (INTERMEDIATE)

Rewrite the following sentences. Use the correct tense and form of the verbs in brackets.

1. If he had taken the morning train, he (reach) Chandigarh by now.
2. The accident victim (survive), if he had been taken to hospital immediately.
3. If you (take) your breakfast, you wouldn't be hungry now.
4. Had I known you were ill, I (visit) you in hospital.
5. If she had been given an assurance, she (continue) in her last job.

6. You would have saved money, if you (buy) the fridge last month.
7. If we'd played better, we (win) the match.
8. Had our party (win), we would have provided a stable government.
9. Had he reached the station on time, he (caught) the train.
10. If you had locked the door properly, no one (enter) your house.

Unit 41

INFINITIVE

To + infinitive verb

There are some verbs such as *want* and *try* in English which can have *to + infinitive verb* in the object position.

(1) She wanted *to work in our factory.*

(2) He tried *to open the door.*

Exercise 1 (intermediate)

Combine the following pairs of sentences. Change sentence *b* into an infinitive in the object position.

1. a. He offered it.
   b. He drove her car.
   He offered to drive her car.
2. a. I want it.
   b. I become a doctor.
3. a. Rakesh promised it.
   b. He finished the work by evening.
4. a. She tried it.
   b. She washed the car.
5. a. I refused it.
   b. I apologised to her.
6. a. You forgot it.
   b. You turned off the fan.
7. a. He failed it.
   b. He passed the driving test.
8. a. He learned it.
   b. He sang.
9. a. I hope something.
   b. I join college next year.
10. a. He can't afford it.
    b. He buys a scooter.

Verb + object + to-infinitive

We can use a noun/pronoun as object after verbs like *want.*

(3) I want to speak *to the Principal.*

(4) I want *you to speak to the Principal.*
(5) I want *her to speak to the Principal.*

Verbs such as *advise, allow, ask, invite, expect, teach, persuade, tell, warm,* etc. require a *noun/pronoun + to-infinitive* after them.

(6) She asked *me to close the door.*
(7) He told me *to receive him at the airport.*
(8) They told *us not to lock our door.*

Note that the negative particle *not* occurs immediately before *to.*

EXERCISE 2 (INTERMEDIATE)

Complete the following sentences using an *object + to-infinitive* after the verbs.

1. (Work hard/Rakesh advised me)
   Rakesh advised me to work hard.
2. (She painted a picture/I asked her) I ....
3. (We worked till 8 o'clock/our manager ordered us) Our manager ....
4. (We didn't cross the fence/The soldier warned us) The soldier ....
5. (Rakhi to watch TV/She invited Rakhi) She ....
6. (Vinod waited for her/Meera told Vinod) Meera ....
7. (I stayed in bed/the doctor advised me) The doctor ....
8. (I took up this job/Hari persuaded me) Hari ....
9. (We finished our assignment/Mrs Kaul reminded us) Mrs Kaul ....
10. (He didn't wait for me/I told him) I ....
11. (She rang you up/I reminded her) I ....
12. (I didn't close the door/she told me) She ....
13. (I sat in the library/the librarian allowed me) The librarian ....
14. (He played cricket/his father taught him) His father ....
15. (She cooked lunch/you didn't tell her) You ....

Adjective + to-infinitive

We use *to-infinitive* after some adjectives.

(9) I am *keen to do this project.*
(10) Vikram is *very eager to meet you.*
(11) He was *glad to meet you.*

(12) It is *boring to live here.*

EXERCISE 3 (INTERMEDIATE)

Combine the following pairs of sentences in such a way that sentence *b* is replaced by to-infinitive in each.

1. a. She is very keen.
   b. She meets you.
   She is very keen to meet you.
2. a. He is sure.
   b. He will pass the examination.
3. a. It is fun for us.
   b. We watch this film.
4. a. She was very happy.
   b. She met you.
5. a. It was clever of him.
   b. He solved the difficult sum.
6. a. It was foolish of him.
   b. He ignored your letter.
7. a. It would look rude.
   b. We ring them up now.
8. a. It was good of her.
   b. She helped you.
9. a. I was careful.
   b. I didn't disclose your secret to her.
10. a. She is sorry.
    b. She bothers you.
11. a. It is difficult for us.
    b. We climb this mountain.
12. a. It is hard.
    b. One believes it.
13. a. Shefali was very glad.
    b. She knew that you were coming.
14. a. He is free.
    b. He leaves this job.
15. a. It was wicked of her.
    b. She used such words.

EXERCISE 4 (ADVANCED)

Rewrite the following sentences using the infinitive.

1. She told me <u>that I shouldn't leave the library.</u>

She told me not to leave the library.

2. He was happy that he had finished the work.
   He was happy to have finished the work.
3. My son was delighted when he learnt that he had passed the entrance examination.
4. She was sorry that she had missed the meeting.
5. It seems that it has rained here.
6. She hopes that she'll finish this novel by tomorrow.
7. I asked her if she could close the door.
8. She promised that she would give me the book.
9. She warned him that he should not drive.
10. Our officer ordered us that we should exercise in the open.
11. She reminded me that I should catch the early morning train.
12. She asked me if I could deliver the lecture in the evening.
13. They would be surprised if they met you.
14. I am sorry that I had to go so soon.
15. He was hurt when he learnt that she had not done his work.
16. She didn't expect that you would come.
17. She promised that she would take the children to the zoo.
18. He was rude when he learnt that he had failed.
19. She would be surprised when she sees you.
20. She hopes that she would become a pilot.

Unit 42

GERUNDS 1

The *-ing* form of a verb sometimes can be used in place of a noun as subject, object, etc. It is then referred to as a *gerund*. For example, consider the following sentences:

(1) *Smoking* can be injurious to health.
(2) *Dancing* can be fun.
(3) I like *sleeping in the afternoon.*
(4) He doesn't like *walking.*

A gerund, though used in the place of a noun, has been derived from a verb. It can be the subject, object or it can be modified by an adverbial.

(5) *Smoking twenty cigarettes a day* can be injurious to health.
(6) *Smoking continuously* can be injurious to health.
(7) Would you mind *closing the door*?
(8) I don't like *her sending flowers to him.*

EXERCISE 1 (ELEMENTARY)

Complete the following sentences. Use the gerund form of the verbs given in brackets.

1. .... is a good pastime. (read)
2. He likes .... cricket. (play)
3. I thought of .... a letter to you (write)
4. .... at others is a bad habit. (shout)
5. It has stopped .... (rain)
6. .... in the morning can keep you fit. (run)
7. .... can be enjoyable. (ride)
8. I like .... (ride), but I don't like .... (run)
9. She doesn't go for .... in the evening. (swim)
10. My father enjoys .... sweets. (eat)
11. .... your head so fast will make you feel dizzy. (turn)
12. His .... is difficult to comprehend. (write)
13. She's good at .... (paint)
14. .... clothes is tiresome. (wash)

15. I'm sorry for .... you. (disturb)
16. .... this bread can be good for you. (eat)
17. I don't like .... this bread. (eat)
18. I enjoy .... in the evening. (work)
19. She loves .... cake. (cook)
20. .... can be fun. (cook)

When a gerund functions as a noun, the possessive form of the noun/ pronoun can be used before it as the subject. Look at the following sentences.

(9a) Meena enjoys it.
(9b) She plays hockey.
(9c) Meena enjoys *playing hockey.*
(10a) She can't bear it.
(10b) He sleeps all evening.
(10c) She can't bear *his sleeping all evening.*

In (9c), the gerund doesn't have a subject as *Meena* and *she* in (9a) and (9b) refer to the same person. So we don't repeat the subject of the gerund if it refers to the subject of the main verb. However (10c) has *his* as the subject of the gerund. Sometimes, we may use the object form of the pronoun and noun, when the gerund is used as the object of the main verb or as complement of an adjective.

(11) She can't bear *him sleeping all evening.*
(12) Manisha can't bear *Mohan's/Mohan sleeping all evening.*

We use the possessive form of the noun/pronoun in the formal style and the object form of the noun/pronoun in the informal style.

EXERCISE 2 (INTERMEDIATE)

Fill in the blanks using the appropriate form of the pronoun in brackets.

1. *She doesn't like <u>him</u> going to an unknown college. (he) informal*
2. *She doesn't like <u>his</u> going to an unknown college. (he) formal*
3. Shefali hates .... wearing a black shirt and tie. (I) formal
4. Shefali hates .... wearing a black shirt and tie (I) informal
5. I can't excuse .... using foul language in class. (she) formal
6. I can't excuse .... using foul language in class (she) informal

7. I remember .... playing football in our ground. (they) informal
8. I remember .... playing football in our ground. (they) formal
9. I can't imagine .... refusing to do this work. (you) informal
10. I can't imagine .... refusing to do this work (you) formal
11. We miss .... singing in the evening. (he) informal
12. We miss .... singing in the evening (he) formal
13. She would certainly mind .... smoking here. (you) informal
14. She would certainly mind .... smoking here. (you) formal
15. I can't understand .... not taking the examination. (she) informal
16. I can't understand .... not taking the examination. (she) formal
17. She regrets .... swearing at you. (he) informal
18. She regrets .... swearing at you. (he) formal
19. We now remember .... visiting us every weekend. (you) informal
20. We now remember .... visiting us every weekend. (you) formal
21. Please excuse .... reading from your book. (we) informal
22. Please excuse .... reading from your book (we) formal
23. The English teacher has agreed to .... attending her evening classes. (you) informal
24. The English teacher has agreed to .... attending her evening classes. (you) formal
25. I can't imagine .... having done it. (she) formal

There are many verbs in English which are followed by only the gerund, e.g. *admit, appreciate, avoid, consider, delay, deny, dislike, enjoy, explain, feel like, finish, forgive, keep, mention, mind, practice, resist, stop, can't resist, can't help, can't stand etc.*

Exercise 3 (intermediate)

Rewrite the following sentences using the word (s) given in brackets.

1. He loves (eat) hot food.
   He loves eating hot food.
2. I can't stand (she, snore) at night.
   I can't stand her snoring at night.
3. She kept on (shout) for half an hour.
4. She does mind (you, smoke) in her house.
5. I enjoy (walk) in the evening.

6. I dislike (she, watch) TV the whole evening.
7. She remember (you, tell) her to ring up Rakesh.
8. I appreciate (you, work) so hard.
9. He denies (have) taken it home.
10. She has already finished (read) this book.
11. I feel like (jump) into the pool.
12. You won't mind (I, sit) next to you.
13. I really don't understand (she, writing) to the Director.
14. I insisted on (he, leave) the room after he behaved in such a manner.
15. She loves (sleep) on the floor.
16. I don't like (they, come) late to office.
17. I dread (meet) him tomorrow in school.
18. I regret (speak) to you rudely.
19. She considered (open) the hotel but it required a lot of money.
20. I remember (return) the books to you.

Unit 43

GERUNDS 2

A gerund can be used as an uncountable noun after prepositions. A preposition is usually followed by a noun. Therefore, the gerund can also occur after a preposition.

(1) She doesn't know anything *about making films.*
(2) He insisted *on doing it* himself.

Exercise 1 (advanced)

Fill in the blanks with the correct preposition and the gerund form of the verb given in brackets.

1. I don't approve .... your .... fast (drive).
   I don't approve of your driving fast.
2. Have you ever thought .... the Civil Services examination? (take)
   Have you ever thought of taking the Civil Services examination?
3. He apologised .... rude to me. (be)
4. I'm keen .... the swimming club. (join)
5. He's interested .... for your company. (work)
6. She succeeded .... a job for herself. (find)
7. My father insisted .... him more work. (give)
8. Are you thinking .... a pet? (buy)
9. Many of us are afraid .... near animals. (go)
10. We decided .... him time. (give)
11. I'm looking forward .... her. (meet)
12. She always dreams .... a police officer. (become)
13. Excuse me .... you, but there is an important message for you. (interrupt)
14. I don't feel .... today. (go out)
15. She is very good .... languages. (learn)
16. I'm fed up .... here. (work)
17. Are you interested .... in our school for a month? (teach)
18. All of us are excited .... on vacation in July. (go)
19. Do you know anything .... ? (fly)
20. Meera apologised .... not .... me .... (ring up)

There are some verbs which have the structure verb + object + preposition + gerund.

(3) They *warned him against entering the house.*

(4) He *prevented her from jumping over the wall.*

Some of these verbs can be used in the passive.

(5) He was warned against entering the house.

Exercise 2 (advanced)

Combine the following pairs of sentences in such a way that sentence *b* is changed into a gerund.

1. a. Mukesh thanked me for ....
   b. I had helped him.
   Mukesh thanked me for helping him.
2. a. He loves ....
   b. He eats hot food.
   He loves eating hot food.
3. a. She believes in ....
   b. She works hard.
4. a. I must congratulate you on ....
   b. You have passed the examination with an 'A' grade.
5. a. She thanked me for ....
   b. I sent her flowers.
6. a. Please forgive me ....
   b. I didn't send you books.
7. a. I've already finished ....
   b. I wrote letters.
8. a. I love ....
   b. I watch TV in the evening.
9. a. I regret ....
   b. I spoke rudely to you.
10. a. Mr Kapoor thanked me for ....
    b. I had received him at the station.
11. a. I'm looking forward to ....
    b. I attend your wedding tomorrow.
12. a. She warned me against ....
    b. I might have entered the old house.
13. a. We stopped everyone from ....
    b. They would cross the flooded road.
14. a. He succeeded in ....
    b. He made a century.
15. a. I enjoy ....
    b. I sing.

16. a. Have you finished .... ?
    b. You were taking a bath.
17. a. I don't mind ....
    b. I get up early in the morning.
18. a. All the students are excited about ....
    b. They are going to the seaside.
19. a. He insisted on ....
    b. He bought me a cycle.
20. a. She accused me of ....
    b. I might have stolen her dress.

A gerund can be used as the subject of a verb.

(6) *Smoking* is injurious to health.

(7) *Her singing in the morning* disturbs us.

EXERCISE 3 (INTERMEDIATE)

Fill in the blanks with the gerund form of the verb given within brackets.

1. .... can be dangerous. (drive fast)
   Driving fast can be dangerous.
2. I heard a lot of .... in the evening (shout)
   I heard a lot of shouting in the evening.
3. Can I do the .... here. (iron)
4. .... intelligent is an advantage. (be)
5. .... keeps you healthy. (run in the morning)
6. We all enjoyed .... (she, sing)
7. .... is real fun. (ride)
8. .... can be dangerous. (fly planes)
9. I'm sorry for .... (disturb you)
10. She's good at .... (repair TV sets)
11. Would you mind .... ? (leave early)
12. What do you know about .... ? (make dolls)
13. .... is a good exercise. (swim in the morning)
14. I like .... (swim in the evening).
15. .... can be difficult. (cut metal)
16. .... is not good for health. (sleep late)
17. Are you interested in .... ? (work for us)
18. .... is a good pastime. (read novels)
19. .... woke me up. (she shouted)
20. I don't mind .... (get up early)

21. .... is really enjoyable. (travel by train)
22. I don't mind .... (travel by train)
23. Have you finished .... the utensils? (clean)
24. .... makes me tired. (teach for six hours)
25. .... was appreciated by everyone. (they sang)

A *gerund* after prepositions such as *before, after, on* and *without* can function as an *adverbial phrase.*

(8) I switched off the fan *before leaving the room.*
(9) *After passing class 12,* she joined a medical college.
(10) Sunil left *without eating anything.*

EXERCISE 4 (ADVANCED)

Combine the following pairs of sentences by changing the second sentence of each pair into an adverbial phrase. Use the preposition given within brackets at the end of the second sentence. You can use the adverbial phrase either in the beginning or in the end of a sentence.

1. a. He went home.
   b. He bought some potatoes. (after)
2. a. She rang up her mother.
   b. She reached the airport. (on)
3. a. He had dinner with his neighbours.
   b. He went to the railway station. (before)
4. a. She was taken to hospital.
   b. She was hit by a car. (after)
5. a. Monica went to England.
   b. She couldn't meet her parents. (without)
6. a. Open the door.
   b. Don't disturb him. (without)
7. a. My father sent me money.
   b. He received my letter. (after)
8. a He got 'A' grade.
   b. He didn't work hard. (without)
9. a. I realised I had left the ticket at home.
   b. I reached the airport. (on)
10. a. Leena met her husband.
    b. She passed the B.A. degree. (before)

Unit 44

INFINITIVES OR GERUNDS

There are certain verbs such as *attempt, begin, cannot/can't bear, cease, commence, continue, hate, intend, like, love, prefer, cannot/ can't stand,* and *start* after which we can use a *to-infinitive* or the gerund without any difference in meaning.

(1a) I like *eating mangoes.* Or
(1b) I like *to eat mangoes.*
(2a) I can't bear *working in this atmosphere.* Or
(2b) I can't bear *to work in this atmosphere.*
(3a) It started *raining in the evening.* Or
(3b) It started *to rain in the evening.*

However, there are certain restrictions on the use of the gerund after the verbs mentioned above. We do not use the gerund form of stative verbs like *know* and *understand* after *begin, cease* and *continue.*

(4a) I *began to understand* her plan. (✓)
not
(4b) I *began understanding* her plan. (×)

We also do not use the gerund after the progressive forms of *begin, cease, continue,* or *start.*

(5a) I'm *beginning to realise* your problem. (✓)
not
(5b) I'm *beginning realising* your problem. (×)

EXERCISE 1 (INTERMEDIATE)

Fill in the blanks with the to-infinitive/the gerund form of the verb within brackets. Give both the forms where they are possible.

1. I intend .... a bookshop. (open)
2. She can't bear .... an emotional film. (watch)
3. Do you prefer .... by train? (travel)
4. I'm beginning .... your difficulty. (understand)
5. I've begun .... you well. (know)
6. I'm intending .... her tomorrow. (visit)

7. I intend .... her tomorrow. (visit)
8. We've just started .... our breakfast. (eat)
9. I was starting .... the picture (paint)
10. She was beginning .... the board when we reached there. (address)
11. Madhavi loves .... TV in the evening. (watch)
12. He hates .... in the morning. (get up)
13. I like .... tennis in the evening. (play)
14. She is starting .... the violin. (play)
15. I had just started .... attendance when the Principal entered the room. (take)

We only use *to*+infinitive after the expressions *would like, would prefer*, and *would love.*

(6) I *would like to meet* him again.
(7) I *would love to read* this book.
(8) *Would* you *like to have* some tea?

We use the gerund after the verbs *dislike, enjoy, finish, stop, suggest.*

(9) I *don't mind travelling* by train.
(10) It *has stopped raining* outside.

EXERCISE 2 (INTERMEDIATE)

Fill in the blanks with either the *to*-infinitive or the gerund. Use the verb given within brackets.

1. She would like .... this letter. (read)
2. She dislikes .... a bath in the morning. (take)
3. I have finished .... letters. (write)
4. I would love .... with you. (play)
5. I love .... cards. (play)
6. I hate .... a match. (lose)
7. I would prefer .... by train. (go)
8. I don't like .... in the afternoon. (shop)
9. Do you mind .... by bus? (travel)
10. I very much enjoy .... classical music. (listen to)

In the case of some verbs, it is possible to use either *to*-infinitive or gerund after them. However, there will be different meanings expressed by them.

- *Remember, forget* and *regret*: *to*-infinitive refers to the past or future and the gerund refers to the past.

(11) Remember to attend the meeting tomorrow.
(12) I don't remember attending the meeting you're referring to.

- *Try* + ———: *try to* means to *make an effort* and *try + gerund* means *experimenting.*

(13) She tried to hold the glass.
(14) I tried holding the glass on my head.

Exercise 3 (advanced)

Fill in the blanks with the correct forms of the verbs in brackets.

1. I told them (stop) (play) in my garden.
2. I advised him (take) rest for two days and then start (walk) with a stick.
3. I remember (she, ask) us (meet) her in the library.
4. I don't mind (take) lunch now but I don't want (eat) ice cream.
5. Would you like (have) the lunch now?
6. I enjoy (read) in the evening but now I would prefer (watch) TV.
7. I'm sorry for (knock) at your door but I want (inform) you that there'll be a power cut tomorrow.
8. He hopes (become) an army officer.
9. I would like (he, start) (prepare) tea.
10. All of us suspected him of (try) (steal) the library books.
11. Do you remember (I, ask) you (close) the door?
12. I regret (say) that the Principal wants (you, leave) the class immediately.
13. Please remember (meet) my clerk at the railway station.
14. I want (you, study) hard.
15. He is sure (finish) the work by evening; therefore, there is no need (remind) him every now and then.
16. I'm glad (know) that he would like (visit) us.
17. Try (open) the lock with this key.
18. I saw (she, try) (cross) the road.
19. You must remember (remind) Harinder (switch off) the fans before leaving the house.
20. She likes (cook) food so I don't understand (she, refuse) (cook) fish.
21. She's free (leave) this job but tell her that I want (speak) to her before she submits her resignation.
22. I appreciate (you, speak) to the General Manager and (request) him (expedite) our case.

23. I couldn't resist (tell) him that he should have tried (prepare) the proposal.
24. It has started (rain) and therefore (drive) will be a bit difficult.
25. I remember (be) in school when I was five years old. We liked (read) aloud in the main hall of the school.

Unit 45

DIRECT AND INDIRECT SPEECH 1

There are two ways of reporting what people say:

One is direct speech. We use the direct speech to quote the actual words used by another person in spoken communication. In writing, we indicate direct speech by the use of quotation marks and other marks of punctuation.

The other is indirect speech. We use indirect speech to report what another person says or said. While using indirect speech, we may make changes in pronouns, adverbs, tenses etc.

For example, if someone called Rahul said:

I'm washing clothes

there are two ways of telling someone else what Rahul said.

- You can repeat Rahul's words, which is called *direct speech*:
  (1) Rahul said, 'I'm washing clothes.'
- You can report what Rahul said in your own words, which is called *indirect speech*.
  (2) Rahul said (that) he was washing clothes.

Direct Speech

- When we use direct speech, we usually use reporting verbs such as *say*, *tell* and *ask*.
- When the subject and the reporting verb come at the beginning of a sentence, we use a comma after the reporting verb, or after the object (if there is an object) and put the reported words within inverted commas (' ').
  (3) Vanita said, 'I will bring the book tomorrow.'
  (4) Mohan asked, 'What time will we begin the exam?'
  (5) She said, 'Open the door, please.'
  (6) Mary exclaimed, 'What a beautiful painting!'
- When the subject and the reporting verb come after what is said, we put a comma after the second inverted comma.

(7) 'I have finished reading this book,' said Mukesh.
(8) 'Close the window, please,' said Mariam.

- If there is a question mark or an exclamation mark at the end of the quotation, we do not use a comma after the quotation.

(9) 'When do we leave?' Sonali asked.
(10) 'What a surprise!' she exclaimed.

EXERCISE 1 (ELEMENTARY)

Use inverted commas and other punctuation marks in the following sentences.

1. Mohan said I am going to Delhi tomorrow.
2. It's lying on the table said she.
3. Are you keeping well Ramesh asked.
4. Drive as fast as you can said Sunita.
5. What a beautiful day it is she exclaimed.
6. Where were you he asked me.
7. We saw this film last week John said.
8. Meera said to me I saw you last night.
9. I saw you last night Meera said.
10. Meenakshi asked me who showed you my house.
11. Rajan said he is not keeping well.
12. He is not keeping well said Rajan.
13. What's the time Gopal asked.
14. Gopal exclaimed what a fool I've been.
15. Shall we leave now she asked.
16. Farida asked is that his car.
17. What a surprise he exclaimed.
18. Rehman said I was sleeping in the evening.
19. She exclaimed what a lovely house you have!
20. She said please take me to my father.

INDIRECT SPEECH

Pronoun changes in indirect speech

- First person pronouns (I, my, me, our, us) are changed according to who the speaker is:

(11a) Meena said, '*I* have given him *my* book.'
(11b) Meena said that *she* had given him *her* book.
(12a) You said 'I am buying a car.'
(12b) You said that *you* were buying a car.

- Second person pronouns (you, your) are changed according to the listener or the person who is addressed.
  - (13a) Anita said to *me*, '*Your* car is parked next to *your* scooter.'
  - (13b) Anita told me that *my* car was parked next to *my* scooter.
  - (14a) Anita said to her, 'Your father is waiting for you.'
  - (14b) Anita told her that her father was waiting for her.
- Third person pronouns (he, she, it, they, him, her, them, his, their) remain unchanged.
  - (15a) Our English teacher said, 'All students must bring their books.'
  - (15b) Our English teacher said that all students must bring their books.

Adverbial changes in indirect speech

Adverbials of time and place change in indirect speech as follows:

Direct speech	Indirect speech
this/that	these/those
here	there
today	that day
tonight	that night
yesterday	the previous day/the day before
tomorrow	the next day/the following day
last week/year	the previous week/year
next week/year	the following week/year

(16a) Rishi said to me, 'I reached Mumbai yesterday.'

(16b) Rishi told me that he had reached Mumbai the previous day.

Reporting verb in the present

If the reporting verb is in the present, the tenses and adverbials of the reported speech are usually the same as those used in the original statement.

(17a) She says, 'I'm going to college tomorrow.'

(17b) She says that she's going to college tomorrow.

(18a) He says, 'I will answer the phone.'
(18b) He says that he will answer the phone.

EXERCISE 2 (ELEMENTARY)

Change the following into indirect speech.

1. She says, 'I have already read this novel.'
2. Mary says, 'Sadhana is sitting in the library.'
3. He says, 'I've typed those letters.'
4. Captain Singh says, 'I've flown this plane for five years.'
5. Monica says, 'You've a wonderful house.'
6. She has just told me, 'The Prime Minister has arrived at the airport.'
7. She says, 'I'm very sorry.'
8. He has just told me, 'They have already finished the work.'
9. My mother says, 'You can call your friends next week.'
10. She's always telling people, 'I drive very well.'
11. 'I work 12 hours a day,' says Mr Kapur.
12. 'My father is a cabinet minister,' Karan has just told me.
13. 'I've got many friends,' says Tanya.
14. She says, 'Meera is coming to the party.'
15. He says, 'I'm not feeling well.'

Reporting verb in the past

When the reporting verb is in the past, we usually move the reported clauses 'one tense back'. As a general rule, we should follow these:

Direct speech	**Indirect speech**
works	worked
is working	was working
has/have worked	had worked
worked	had worked
shall/will work	should/would work
could/should/would work	could/should/would have worked

(19a) I said, 'She is sleeping inside.'
(19b) I said that she was sleeping inside.
(20a) She told me, 'I worked till 11 o'clock yesterday.'
(20b) She told me that she had worked till 11 o'clock the previous day.

Exercise 3 (intermediate)

Change the following into indirect speech.

1. Kunal told me, 'I'll go to Ahmedabad next week.'
2. He said, 'I could help you.'
3. She said, 'I am living in Amritsar.'
4. Monica told me, 'I was sitting in my room.'
5. Rakesh said, 'She hasn't finished her homework.'
6. She told me, 'You should work hard.'
7. He told me, 'I shall see you tomorrow.'
8. She told me, 'I finished reading this novel last week.'
9. Anima said, 'I don't know what she'll do.'
10. Vinod told me, 'You can come with me.'
11. She told me, 'I like your new car.'
12. He said, 'I kept it here in the cover last week.'
13. The teacher told me, 'I'll teach you Shakespeare next week.'
14. Farida said, 'I'm going to buy a new house.'
15. Kunal said, 'I woke up at 6 o'clock yesterday.'
16. Punit said, 'We came back to the hostel very late last night.'
17. She said, ' The film was very interesting.'
18. He said, 'I was not well yesterday.'
19. Ashish said, 'This book is very expensive.'
20. Mohinder said, 'I slept for four hours in the afternoon.'

We do not change the tense in the reported clause even when the reporting verb is in the past.

- If the reported speech describes a universal truth or a habitual fact:

  (21a) Our teacher said, 'The earth revolves around the sun'.
  (21b) Our teacher said the earth revolves around the sun.

Exercise 4 (advanced)

Change the following into indirect speech.

1. The officer said, 'She must join duty tomorrow.'
2. She told me, 'If I go to Chennai, I'll get a shirt for you.'
3. Meera said, 'I waited for you till six in the evening. When you didn't turn up, I rang up your home.'
4. Avinash said to me, 'When I reached the station, I found that the train had already left.'
5. The clerk said to me, 'All the trains for Varanasi run in the evening and therefore you can buy your ticket in the afternoon.'

6. The doctor said to me, 'You have gained ten kilos and you're not doing any exercise in the morning.'
7. The shopkeeper said to me, 'I can get you the best quality sugar tomorrow. You may take it in the evening.'
8. My father said, 'You must work hard if you want to join the civil services.'
9. The officer said, 'I caught you red-handed and you're saying that you didn't cross the red light.'
10. The new clerk said to me, 'I worked in the railways for five years but had to leave because I couldn't travel fifteen days a month.'
11. My brother said, 'The film that I saw yesterday on television was an award-winning film.'
12. Sarika said to Anita, 'It is very hot in Lucknow in summer. Therefore, you should visit Lucknow in November.'
13. Monish said, 'If you feel cold, I'll close the window.'
14. Pradip said, 'The plane will leave in twenty minutes; so I should leave now.'
15. Asha said to me, 'As Nilofer left Mumbai yesterday, she should reach Guwahati tomorrow.'

Unit 46

DIRECT AND INDIRECT SPEECH 2

QUESTIONS

Yes-no questions

- We use *asked, enquired, wondered*, or *wanted to know* as the reporting verb.
- We use *if* or *whether* after the reporting verb.
- The inversion of subject-auxiliary in yes-no questions changes to the statement word order.

(1a) She told me, 'Are you reading this book?'
(1b) She asked me if/whether I was reading that book.
(2a) He told me, 'Did you meet Rahul at the station?'
(2b) He wanted to know if/whether I had met Rahul at the station.

EXERCISE 1 (INTERMEDIATE)

Change the following sentences into indirect speech.

1. 'Did you study hard for the exam?' she said.
2. Vinayak told me, 'Have you seen this film?'
3. 'Do you always travel by car?' Ramesh said.
4. Mohini told Rita, 'Will you teach us Shakespeare next year?'
5. 'Have you ever been to Kashmir, Kamini?' I said.
6. She told me, 'Did you write this article?'
7. Rohan told her, 'Is it raining outside?'
8. Meenakshi told him, 'Will you attend office tomorrow?'
9. 'Did you visit Chandigarh last year, Sarada?' Damini said.
10. 'Can I use your car, Varoon?' Karan said.
11. The English teacher said to me, 'Did you see Manohar yesterday?'
12. She said to me, 'Are you enjoying yourself?'
13. Hari said to me, 'May I take leave tomorrow?'
14. Sushmita said, 'Have you chained the dog, Abhishek?'
15. Ashi said, 'Did you switch off the fan before leaving the room, Meetu?'
16. Garima said to me, 'Are you watching TV?'
17. I said, 'Karishma, have you accepted this assignment?'

18. My father said to me, 'Will you take Roomi to the doctor?'
19. Mira said to her husband, 'Are you going to Lucknow tomorrow?'
20. My neighbour said to me, 'Can you hear a noise?'

Wh-questions

- We may use *asked, enquired* or *wanted to know* as the reporting verb.
- The wh-word (what, why, how, etc.) is used as a link between the reporting verb and the reported wh-question.
- The inversion of subject-auxiliary in the wh-question changes to statement word order.

(3a) She said to me, 'When are you teaching us Byron?'
(3b) She asked me when I was teaching them Byron.
(4a) Mohit said, 'Where did they park the car?'
(4b) Mohit wanted to know where they had parked the car.

EXERCISE 2 (INTERMEDIATE)

Change the following into indirect speech.

1. He said, 'When will dinner be ready?'
2. Mohini said, 'Why are you crying, Rekha?'
3. I said, 'How can I reach the port?'
4. She said to me, 'Where did you keep the box?'
5. Akram said, 'How will she reach here?'
6. Faryal said, 'Where did they go last week?'
7. Mala said to me, 'When can you send the books to me?'
8. Rahul said, 'What are you looking for?'
9. He said to me, 'When will you come again?'
10. She said to me, 'Why didn't you speak to my mother?'
11. Manu said, 'Where do they live?'
12. Vijay said to me, 'How is your mother?'
13. Hema said, 'Where have I kept my spectacles?'
14. Ashok said to me, 'How long have you worked in this office?'
15. She said, 'How far is the airport from the city?'
16. He said to me, 'What did you tell my father?'
17. My father said to me, 'When do you want me to reach the station?'
18. She said, 'How much will this cap cost?'
19. He said to me, 'Who are you looking for?'
20. He said, 'How much does it weigh?'

Unit 47

DIRECT AND INDIRECT SPEECH 3

The imperative

- We report the imperative with a suitable verb + *to* infinitive. The reporting verb may match the function of the imperative (*asking, telling, requesting, commanding, advising,* etc.)
- When we report a negative imperative, we put *not* or *never* before the *to*-infinitive.

(1a) 'Please open the door', she said to me.
(1b) She requested me to open the door.
(2a) 'Don't open the door', she said to me.
(2b) She asked me not to open the door.

Exercise 1 (intermediate)

Change the following into indirect speech. Use the simple past of the verbs in brackets.

1. She said to him, 'Get me a glass of water'. (ask)
2. She said to him, 'Close the window, please.' (request)
3. The doctor said to the patient, 'Don't take cold water.' (advise)
4. 'Don't enter the room,' the English teacher said to Ajay. (warn)
5. 'Don't play loud music in your room,' Anshu said to Nirupama. (ask)
6. 'Remember to send an e-mail to Arjun,' he asked me. (remind)
7. Rajneesh said to me, 'Carry this box in your car, please.' (request)
8. He said to me, 'Don't wait for me.' (tell)
9. The teacher said to the class, 'Open the book on page seventy two.' (ask)
10. She said to him, 'Don't even do it again.' (warn)
11. My mother said to me, 'Wash your hair.' (tell)
12. He said to me, 'Wait here till I come.' (ask)
13. Monisha said to me, 'Give me your mobile, please.' (request)
14. 'Don't eat this rice,' Rohan said to me. (advise)
15. The air hostess said to me, 'Keep the aisle seat vacant, please.' (request)
16. He said to me, 'Don't boil the tea.' (tell)
17. The commanding officer said to the Captain, 'Fire at once.' (order)
18. The officer said to the soldier, 'Don't leave for your platoon tomorrow.' (command)

19. The teacher said to the students, 'Don't make noise.' (ask)
20. My father said to me, 'Take the car out of the garage.' (tell)

Offers, suggestions, requests for advice

We make offers and suggestions with *shall* or *should*.

(3a) She said to me, 'Shall I call him?'
(4a) She said to me, 'Should I phone him?'

We can change (3a) and (4a) into indirect speech in two ways.

(3b) She asked/wanted to know if/whether she should call him.
(3c) She asked/wanted to know whether to call him. (not *if to*)
(4b) She asked/wanted to know if/whether she should phone him.
(4c) She asked/wanted to know whether to phone him.

Exercise 2 (Intermediate)

Change the following into indirect speech in two ways.

1. She said, 'Shall I help you?'
2. She said to him, 'Shall I cook the lunch?'
3. Meera said to me, 'Should I get the car for you?'
4. Madhu said to me, 'Shall I invite her to lunch?'
5. Tanya said to Karan, 'Shall I give you the letter now?'
6. He said, 'Shall I heat it now?'
7. My wife said to me, 'Should we start now?'
8. She said to her husband, 'Shall I bake the cake tomorrow?'
9. He said to me, 'Shall I close the door?'
10. Seema said to Akash, 'Shall we meet tomorrow?'

Exercise 3 (Advanced)

Change the following into indirect speech.

1. Anita said to me, 'I don't know the way to the City Plaza. Could you ask the traffic policeman the way?'
2. The teacher said to the student, 'Why didn't you do your homework? Go and report to the class teacher.'
3. She said to me, 'Are you coming to college tomorrow? Everyone wants to meet you.'
4. My sister said to me, 'I am very thirsty. Get me a glass of water, please.'

5. My mother said to me, 'I'm very tired. Shall I wash the utensils tomorrow?'
6. He said to me, 'Have you got any soap? I want to have a bath.'
7. Shailaja said to Vijay, 'Where have you put the book? I want to study English literature.'
8. My father said to me, 'Go to the post office and post these letters. These letters must reach my branch office next week.'
9. Kunal said to Vishal, 'Would you have dinner with us tomorrow? We are having a party tomorrow.'
10. The officer said to the soldier, 'Take the jeep to the airport and bring the Commanding Officer here. I shall wait for him in the mess.'
11. She said to me, 'I'm going to the station. Shall I buy your ticket also?'
12. My mother said to her friend, 'The shops close at 8 o'clock. Shall we go to the market now?'
13. He said to me, 'When are you leaving for Delhi? I want to give you a small packet for my brother.'
14. Nora said to Ali, 'I usually go to the office by bus. Do you take the morning bus to the office?'
15. She said to me, 'I went to sleep at 10 o'clock yesterday. I don't remember when you returned home.'
16. The Principal said to me, 'I want you to join the debating club. Can you see Mr Kapoor tomorrow?'
17. My friend said to my father, 'Can I speak to Harish? I'm speaking from Mumbai.'
18. The shopkeeper said, 'May I help you? We have got some fresh dry fruit today.'
19. He said to me, 'Have you ever been to Chandigarh? It's a very beautiful city.'
20. Rohit said to Raju, 'Get me some medicines, please. I'm not feeling too well today.'

Unit 48

ACTIVE AND PASSIVE VOICE 1

General information about the passive

- In the active voice, the subject of the verb is the person or thing that does the action.

  (1) *The Prime Minister has visited* Lucknow.
  (2) *Vijay constructed* this house in 1986.

- In the passive, the subject (or in other words the object in the active) has the focus. The action is 'done' to the subject in the passive.

  (3) Lucknow *has been visited* by the Prime Minister.
  (4) *This house was constructed* in 1986.

- We can only passivise transitive verbs. Intransitive and linking verbs cannot be passivised.

  (5) a. She *is typing* a letter. (*type* is a transitive verb).
  b. A letter *is being typed* by her.
  (6) It *is raining* outside. (*rain* is an intransitive verb, so it cannot be passivised)
  (7) My sister is a doctor. (*be* is a linking verb; and therefore cannot be passivised)

- We form the passive by adding *be + past participle*.

  (8) English *is spoken* all over the world.
  (9) This picture *has been drawn* by my younger sister.

- If the subject in the active voice is important as an agent, it is mentioned as *by + agent* in the passive voice.

  (10) The building was inaugurated by the Governor.

- We may have an 'unknown', 'vague' or 'unimportant' subject in the active voice. In such a case, we may not repeat the subject of the active in the passive voice.

  (11a) Someone constructed this building in 1832 (the agent is an unknown 'someone').
  (11b) This building was constructed in 1832.

Passive of the simple present, simple past and will + the main form of the verb

		Active	Passive
simple present	⟶	help(s)	is/are/am helped
simple past	⟶	helped	was/were helped
will + the main form of the verb	→	will + help	will be helped

Exercise 1 (elementary)

Rewrite the following sentences with the passive forms of verbs. Use the tenses suggested in the brackets.

1. You (require) to pay the income tax by 31st March. (simple present)
2. This shop (open) in 1934. (simple past)
3. This issue (discuss) tomorrow. (will +be + past participle)
4. We (invite) to a wedding yesterday. (simple past)
5. The play (stage) next month. (will +be + past participle)
6. She (hit) by a truck in the morning. (simple past)
7. The ball (hit) by Tendulkar to the square leg. (simple present)
8. She (take) to the new hall by the Principal. (simple past)
9. The novel (not publish) this year. (use 'will')
10. All the books (not sell) yesterday. (simple past)
11. The result (declare) on Monday. (use 'will')
12. We (teach) English by Dr Singh. (simple past)
13. All the trains (check) by the station superintendent every day. (simple present)
14. This room (not open) every day. (simple present)
15. The exhibition (inaugurate) by the Vice-chancellor (simple past)
16. The college gate (inaugurate) by the Vice-chancellor tomorrow. (use 'will')
17. She (not allow) to go out of the hospital. (simple present)
18. His mother (kill) in a car accident last month. (simple past)
19. She (not disturb) during the examinations. (use 'will')
20. The fridge (repair) tomorrow. (use 'will')

Exercise 2 (intermediate)

Change the following sentences into passive voice.

1. She serves breakfast at 7 o'clock.
2. Meera read this novel last week.
3. The University will declare the results next week.
4. Someone stole my pen from my pocket.

5. My mother cooks lunch in the morning.
6. The cook prepared this dish yesterday.
7. She will knit a pair or socks for you next week.
8. My sister burnt the food last night.
9. She cut the vegetables into pieces.
10. A truck hit this car last night.
11. We shall post these letters tomorrow.
12. The police caught the thief at the railway station.
13. He published his first novel when he was twenty-five.
14. Mrs Nancy taught us English in class 11.
15. Someone opens this office at 9 o'clock.
16. They didn't pay the rent for two years.
17. People speak Arabic in more than twenty countries.
18. They will not open the shop tomorrow.
19. Our cook didn't cook the food yesterday.
20. The gardener regularly plants flowers in the garden.

Unit 49

ACTIVE AND PASSIVE VOICE 2

Passive of the present continuous and the past continuous

We form the passive form of the continuous forms as follows:

- the present continuous: *be (is/am/are)+being+the past participle*
- the past continuous: *be (was/were) + being + the past participle*

(1a) They are building a new school in Gomti Nagar.
(1b) A new school is being built in Gomti Nagar.
(2a) Someone was washing cars in the evening.
(2b) Cars were being washed in the evening.

Exercise 1 (elementary)

Fill in the blanks with the passive forms of the verbs in the present continuous tense.

1. We .... (question) by the police in the train.
2. The bus .... (park) in the shed.
3. A film .... (make) in this studio these days.
4. All trains .... (withdraw) due to heavy rains.
5. The uniforms .... (distribute) in that hall.
6. The trees .... (cut) to build a new road.
7. Your shirt .... (wash) in the washing machine.
8. The prisoners .... (taken) to the court.
9. The milk .... (boiled).
10. She .... (interview) in the meeting room.

Exercise 2 (elementary)

Fill in the blanks with the passive forms of the verbs in the past continuous form.

1. The train .... (pull) slowly.
2. Many flights .... (cancel) due to heavy fog.
3. The items in the store .... (count) when I reached office.
4. The song .... (sing) when it started raining.
5. The food .... (cook) when the bell rang.
6. Act III .... (stage) when the lights went off.
7. You plan .... (discuss) when the meeting was postponed.

8. The grass .... (cut) when the manager came.
9. The answer books .... (mark) when the Principal came.
10. The dinner .... (serve) when I got the telephone call.

Exercise 3 (intermediate)

Change the following into the passive voice.

1. Someone was cleaning the house in the evening.
2. They are opening the case again.
3. They were making a documentary film when I reached the studio.
4. She is cooking food on the lawn.
5. They are taking the students on a picnic by bus.
6. They are serving food in the main hall.
7. They were distributing tickets at the entrance.
8. Someone was playing loud music at night.
9. They are washing clothes in the garden.
10. They are ironing shirts with a steam iron.
11. They were preparing the report cards in the morning.
12. They are building a new market near the bus stand.
13. They were frying potatoes when I entered the kitchen.
14. They are printing new letter pads.
15. The driver was cleaning our car when we reached home.

Passive of the present perfect and past perfect

We form the passive of the present perfect and past perfect as follows:

- the present perfect: *have/has + been + the past participle*
- the past perfect: *had + been + the past participle*

(3a) Krishna has written this book.
(3b) This book has been written by Krishna.
(4a) She had finished the work before we reached her house.
(4b) The work had been finished by her before we reached her house.

Exercise 4 (intermediate)

Change the following into the passive voice.

1. The government has announced a new tax rate.
2. Someone has broken the front door.
3. This cinema hall has already screened this film.

4. She had already shown us the photographs when you telephoned her.
5. They have built two houses recently near our house.
6. Someone has stolen my scooter.
7. The postman has already delivered the evening mail.
8. Many people have already heard this story.
9. The police have solved the murder mystery.
10. Lightning had struck the house before we reached there.
11. We had already warned them before you came with the court notice.
12. Rushdie has published his latest novel.
13. She has already cooked the dinner.
14. Someone had painted the building.
15. They had employed fifty workers to build the road.
16. She has opened the door.
17. Someone has stopped the train.
18. Someone has demolished the house.
19. The cook has already prepared the meals.
20. The Prime Minister has viewed the parade.

Passive with the modals

The basic modal form in the passive voice is *modal + be/have been + past participle.*

(5a) Mary can do it.
(5b) It can be done by Mary.
(6a) Someone might have already despatched lette
(6b) Letters might have already been despatched.

Exercise 5 (intermediate)

Change the following into the passive voice.

1. Someone will drive you to the station.
2. We must obey the law.
3. Someone must have already written a book on tribal languages.
4. You can buy such a pen anywhere.
5. The police might have caught the thief by now.
6. Someone must have already received her at the airport.
7. One cannot solve this mystery.
8. They could have successfully conducted the test last month.
9. We will conduct the meeting tomorrow.
10. You must take her to the doctor.

11. Somebody must have stolen my watch while I was standing at the bus stand.
12. They should not buy this house.
13. Someone must account for every rupee.
14. Someone could have opened the door in the evening.
15. She must have collected the clothes.

The passive of sentences with ditransitive verbs

A ditransitive verb has two objects – the indirect object and the direct object. If we change such an active sentence into the passive, it is possible to get two passive versions. However, it is more usual to make the indirect object the subject of the passive voice.

(7a) Someone gave *me an apple.*
(7b) *I* was given an apple.
(7c) *An apple* was given (to) me.

EXERCISE 6 (INTERMEDIATE)

Change the following sentences into the passive voice. Use the italicised indirect object in the active sentence as a subject in the passive.

1. She asked *me* a question in the class.
2. I will give *him* the book tomorrow.
3. She taught *us* French in class 9.
4. Someone recommended *her* to another doctor.
5. Someone has already paid *the plumber* his monthly wages.
6. Our English teacher told *us* to attend the class on Sunday.
7. They requested *Kamlesh* to deliver a lecture on Wednesday.
8. They have already given *her* permission for the journey.
9. The Principal allowed *me* to take the examination again.
10. They showed *the guests* the new college building.
11. Someone asked *them* a difficult question.
12. She gave *Vinod* enough money to visit Japan.
13. They will allow *each girl* to wear her personal clothes once a week.
14. You can ask *him* to proceed on leave.
15. They have given *him* a new project.

Unit 50

ACTIVE AND PASSIVE VOICE 3

The passive with verbs such as *say* and *believe*

Sometimes we need to be sure of our facts. For example, we might say:

(1a) The President will visit the USA next week.

If we are not sure of the facts, we may say:

(1b) It is said/expected that the President will visit the USA next week.

(1c) The President is expected to visit the USA next week.

We can express caution in three ways, with:

- *It* + passive form of the verb + *that* clause with verbs such as *agree, believe, consider, decide, hope, know, say.* For example,

  (2) It is hoped that the prices will not rise further.

- *There* + passive form of the verb + *to be* with verbs such as *allege, believe, fear, know, report, say, suppose, think.* For example,

  (3) There is believed to be a monster in the jungle.

- Subject + passive form of the verb + to-infinitive with verbs such as *allege, believe, consider, say.* For example,

  (4) Mukesh is alleged to have stolen a car.

Exercise 1 (Advanced)

Fill in the blanks with *It/there/a noun/+ the passive form of the verb* in brackets.

1. .... that India will be an economic power soon. (expect)
2. .... that the Parliament will pass the bill. (hope)
3. .... to be a lot of oil in this area. (say)
4. .... to have made this picture. (think)
5. .... to be a lot of coal in India. (believe)
6. .... that Mr Sharma will be the new Chief Minister. (hope)
7. .... that Mr Bhargava is the wisest man in the village. (know)

8. .... to be a rise in the prices of new plots of land. (suppose)
9. .... to have committed the crime. (think)
10. .... that there are no survivors. (fear)
11. .... to know the latest developments in history. (say)
12. .... that the temperature of the earth is rising. (think)
13. .... to be an expert in this field. (consider)
14. .... to have the largest democracy in the world. (suppose)
15. .... that there was a great civilisation existing in this area. (believe)

Unit 51

PREPOSITIONS 1

PREPOSITIONS OF PLACE/ POSITION

A. ***In, at* and *on***

Study the following figures and expressions.

in

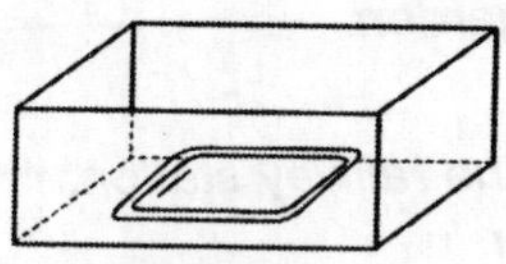

in the box

in the glass

in the house

(1) There is a biscuit *in the box.*

(2) There is some milk *in the glass/cup.*

(3) She is singing *in the house/in the garden.*

at

at the bus stand/station

at the window/door

(4) She met me *at the bus stand/station.*

(5) There is a lady standing *at the door/at the window.*

on

on the window

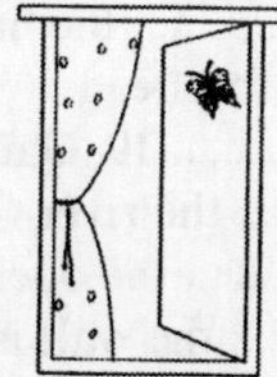

on the door

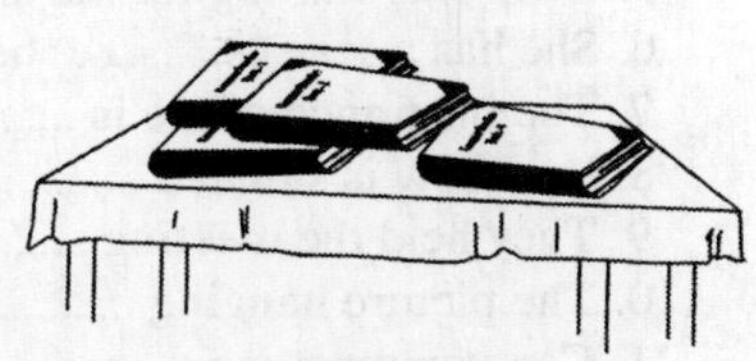

on the table

(6) The books are lying *on the table.*

(7) There is a butterfly *on the window/on the door.*

We also use *in* before the name of a continent, a state, a town, a city, or a village.

(8) He was born *in Germany.*
(9) Rakesh lives *in Coimbatore.*

We use *in* before the name of a road, a street, a room, and any other enclosed space big enough to be all around a person.

(10) Meena lives *in Victoria Street.*
(11) It was dark *in her office/in the cinema hall.*
(12) Manish was sleeping *in the garden.*

We use *at* to describe a position.

(13) Khalil was waiting for me *at the railway station.*
(14) She was standing *at the door.*

We use *at* for a house or an address.

(15) He lives *at 32, Lower Circular Road.*
(16) We were *at home* in the evening.

On has the meaning of 'on the surface'.

(17) We pasted the notice *on the board.*
(18) There is a TV set *on the shelf.*

Exercise 1 (elementary)

Fill in the blanks with *in, at* or *on*.

1. The minister is attending an international conference .... Russia.
2. I'll meet you .... the airport.
3. I met her .... the bus stand.
4. The cows are grazing .... the field.
5. Dilip was waiting for me .... the hall.
6. She has a scar .... her forehead.
7. The insurance office is .... 19, Gandhi Marg.
8. Lucknow is situated .... the river Gomti.
9. They held the meeting .... the open ground.
10. The picture hanging .... the wall is hundred years old.
11. Can you meet me .... the station?
12. They have lived .... Spain for ten years.
13. The train from Delhi arrives .... platform no. 6.
14. There is a fly .... the window.
15. I've kept the books .... the table.
16. Her father is .... hospital.

17. Madhu's flight was delayed. She had to wait .... the airport for five hours.
18. We've kept all the old newspapers .... the big box.
19. She was born .... a village but now she lives .... Mumbai.
20. Krishna was injured in a rail accident last week. He is still .... hospital.
21. Monisha was sitting .... the table .... the class.
22. You may put the books .... the table.
23. It was a very slow train. It stopped .... every station.
24. He speaks fluent Italian. He studied .... Italy for five years.
25. I won't be .... home tomorrow evening.
26. There's enough water .... the kettle. You can put it .... the stove.
27. Mrs Narang teaches .... our college.
28. They live .... Kasturba Gandhi Marg.
29. Their office is situated .... 51, Netaji Subhash Chander Street.
30. I was not feeling well in the morning and so I stayed .... bed the whole day.

B. To, into, onto

To indicates movement towards a building, place, country etc.

(19) They went *to the market* in the evening.

(20) I go *to work* in the morning.
(21) I have been *to Nepal* twice.

Into indicates movement into a room, building, river etc.

(22) She ran *into the room*.

(23) He dived *into the river.*

Onto indicates movement into a bus, train etc.

(24) We got *onto the bus.*

Onto also indicates the place towards which someone or something is directed.

(25) Sanjeev climbed *onto the roof.*
(26) He came out of the hotel *onto the street.*

EXERCISE 2 (INTERMEDIATE)

Fill in the blanks with *to, into, onto.*

1. She had some work in the bank.
   She went inside the bank. She went into the bank.
2. He has visited England many times. He has been .... England many times.
3. Don't wait outside. Come .... the room.
4. They're flying .... New York tomorrow.
5. Tom is not at home. He has gone .... college.
6. She has just entered that building. She has just gone .... that building.
7. I opened the door and went .... the room.
8. They've gone .... the top of the building.
9. The police were chasing the thief but he ran .... a shop.
10. A bird flew .... the room through the door.
11. I'll drive .... the airport.
12. He always walks .... college.
13. She got .... the running train.
14. I'm not feeling well. I'm going .... the doctor.
15. She's just gone .... that house.

C. Over/above, under/below

Over and *above,* and *under* and *below* are sometimes a matter of confusion. They are sometimes used interchangeably but *over* means vertically above and thus indicates nearness.

(27) He had a cut *over his lip.*
(28) We hung our clothes *over the fireplace.*

Above, on the other hand, means *higher than.*

(29) They live in a flat *above ours.*

Similarly, *under* means vertically below and thus indicates *nearness.*

(30) He had a cut *under his lip.*
(31) Our cat sleeps *under my bed.*

Below means lower than.

(32) We saw small houses *below us* from the plane.

D. Behind/beside

The preposition *behind* has the meaning of *at the back* of something and *by* or *beside* has the meaning of *by the side of.*

(33) He left the car *behind the garage.*
(34) He left the car *beside/ by the garage.*

Exercise 3 (advanced)

Fill in the blanks with *above, over, under, below, behind, by* or *beside.* In some cases, more than one preposition can be used.

1. I saw an aeroplane flying .... our house.
2. She has a mole .... her eye.
3. Our college is next to our house. Our college is situated .... our house.
4. We could see the river .... us from the bridge.
5. She was standing next to the door. She was standing .... the door.
6. My cousin's flat is just .... our flat.
7. My book is lying .... the table.
8. She was standing at the back of the stage. She was standing .... the stage.
9. Your letter is lying by the side of the books. Your letter is lying .... the books.
10. The key is lying .... the chair.
11. There are mosquitoes flying .... his head.
12. She has got black patches .... her eyes.
13. There is a house .... those trees.
14. We could see the boats .... the bridge.
15. There is a garden .... our house.

Unit 52

PREPOSITIONS 2

Prepositions of Time

A. At, on and in

At is used with an exact point of time, e.g. *at 5 o'clock, at 9.30, at midnight.* It is also used with meal times e.g. *at lunch, at dinner* and with festivals such as *at X'mas, at Dussehra* etc.

(1) We'll have a meeting *at five o'clock.*
(2) We shall discuss it *at breakfast.*
(3) They're going to have a party *at Diwali.*

On is used with a more general point of time such as *days of the week, dates and parts of the day.*

(4) He gave us a test *on Wednesday.*
(5) His birthday falls *on 18th May.*
(6) I visited her *on Friday evening.*

In is used with *months, years, seasons, centuries* and *parts of the day.*

(7) The elections will be held *in February.*
(8) India won independence *in 1947.*
(9) We have a long vacation *in summer.*

Exercise 1 (elementary)

Fill in the blanks with *at, on* or *in*.

1. The examination will begin .... ten o'clock.
2. All of us meet .... lunch everyday.
3. Our academic session begins .... August and ends .... April.
4. Many scientific instruments were invented .... the nineteenth century.
5. Jawaharlal Nehru was born .... 1889.
6. Her mother is a doctor .... this hospital but she is .... leave at present.
7. This shop was established .... 1982.

8. The old students of our school are meeting .... Christmas.
9. We posted the letter to you .... Tuesday.
10. The evening show begins .... 6.30 .... the evening.
11. They were married .... 1992.
12. I've not seen Mukesh for a few days. I last saw him .... Wednesday.
13. She may not be home .... the morning. You can ring her up .... the evening.
14. She went to Aden .... 1980.
15. Many countries became industrialised .... the twentieth century.
16. The next meeting of the Board will be held .... 25th November.
17. There was a thick mist .... the morning.
18. The train will leave .... four o'clock.
19. Our Managing Director will be retiring .... four months.
20. I usually meet my father .... dinner.
21. Meenakshi's grandmother died .... 1997.
22. Our college starts .... 9 o'clock .... the morning.
23. We get our salaries .... the last working day of the month.
24. I usually drive around town .... night.
25. She visited me .... the afternoon.

B. For and during

We use *for* to express a period of time: *for two years, for five hours, for ten weeks.*

(10) We played football *for two hours.*

(11) They lived in Behrampur *for five years.*

We use *during + noun* to say if something happens continuously or several times in a period of time: *during winter, during the vacation.*

(12) It was very cold *during the winter* last year.

Exercise 2 (intermediate)

Fill in the blanks with *for or during.*

1. She will be in London .... a week.
2. We went to Ooty .... the vacation.
3. She fell asleep .... the movie.
4. They've been in this business .... the last three generations.

5. We met all our friends .... our stay in Dubai.
6. I attended a computer course .... the summer vacation.
7. He worked in our company .... four years before joining your company.
8. We watched TV .... two hours last night.
9. It is not very hot today. It must have rained .... the night.
10. We always play cards .... the lunch break.

C. By and until/till

By is used to express *not later than*.

(13) We'll reach your house *by 5 o'clock*.

(14) She always gets up *by six in the morning.*

Until/till is used to indicate that a situation continues for some time and then stops.

(15) We worked in the library *until 8 o'clock*.

Until/till can also be used to indicate that something did not/will not happen before a particular time.

(16) The library was not opened *till 11 o'clock*.

(17) The guests will not arrive *until five in the evening.*

Exercise 3 (intermediate)

Fill in the blanks with *by* or *until/till*.

1. The tickets are sold .... ten in the morning.
2. They don't sell tickets .... ten in the morning.
3. She has to pay the fees .... Monday.
4. Sorry, I can't join you for tea. I've to reach home .... 5 o'clock.
5. I'll wait here .... she comes back.
6. You can take your dress .... 6 o'clock. We're open .... 8 o'clock.
7. If we leave now, we'll reach Ahmedabad .... lunch.
8. You can work in this room .... Mr Ghai comes back.
9. The train reaches Lucknow .... 8 o'clock.
10. There is no train for Mumbai .... tomorrow morning.

Unit 53

PREPOSITIONS 3

SOME OTHER PREPOSITIONS

By

By is used for means of transport and communication. We use *by* and a noun without the article *the* to indicate means of transport: *by bus, by train, by car, by air.*

(1) We travelled from Delhi to Amritsar *by train.*

(2) They went to Lucknow *by car.*

We may also use *by + a noun* for means of communication.

(3) I received the interview call *by fax.*

(4) You could inform him *by phone.*

We cannot use *by* if we say 'my car/the train/a taxi' etc. We say *in my car, on the train, etc.*

(5) We went to Ludhiana *in a taxi.*

Prepositions of Instrument and Agentive

We use *with + noun phrase* to express the sense of instrument. *With* is usually followed by an inanimate noun.

with a key, with a stone, with a stick

(6) She opened the door *with a key.*

(7) Marina broke the window *with a stone.*

We use *by + noun* to indicate the agentive role of a noun in the passive sentence. The agent is an animate noun.

(8) My brother received a letter today. (active)

(9) A letter was received by my brother today. (passive)

(10) My grandfather constructed this house. (active)

(11) This house was constructed by my grandfather. (passive)

Occasionally, *by+an inanimate noun* may be used for an instrumental function.

(12) The wall was damaged *by the storm.*

With is used to express the meaning of *in the company of* or *together with:*

(13) Ritika went to Shimla *with her father.*

Exercise 1 (intermediate)

Fill in the blanks with *by* or *with*.

1. I received this message .... post.
2. I watched the film .... my friends.
3. They operated the lift .... a single pulley during the power breakdown.
4. He goes to school .... bus.
5. I went to Mauritius .... my family.
6. The building was damaged .... lightning.
7. He received the question papers .... speedpost.
8. She attended the convocation .... her parents.
9. I went to Delhi .... a taxi.
10. I'm going to Udaipur .... air.
11. Her car was hit by .... stone.
12. I got this message .... e-mail.
13. He pulled down the curtain .... a stick.
14. We travelled to Goa .... ship.
15. She went to Paris .... air.

Exercise 2 (advanced)

Fill in the blanks with an appropriate preposition.

1. I saw her standing .... the bus stand.
2. There is some milk .... the packet.
3. There is a big patch .... the wall.
4. When she saw a street dog, she ran .... our house.
5. I have been .... Delhi four times.
6. Her husband started his career .... a small town but now he works .... Chennai.
7. Vijay was hit .... a speeding truck.
8. I saw a helicopter flying .... our college.
9. He goes to school .... the school bus.
10. Our examinations begin .... 15th April.
11. India became a Republic .... 1950.
12. Shailaja lives .... Indira Nagar .... Bangalore.
13. They lived .... Mumbai .... five years.

14. There was a photograph hung .... the bookshelf.
15. We rested .... the tree.
16. We could see the river flowing .... the hotel.
17. We'll meet .... lunch and discuss this issue.
18. I received this gift .... post.
19. She visited .... Channai .... the winter vacation.
20. Mr Khan goes .... office .... car.
21. The main building is hidden .... the trees.
22. We took tea .... the interval.
23. It is very cold .... winter .... Shimla.
24. They live .... 20, Modern Town.
25. My grandmother died .... 1989.
26. The plane reaches Hyderabad .... 5 o'clock.
27. You can come to my office. I'll be there .... 6 o'clock.
28. As she was ill, she was taken .... the hospital .... an ambulance.
29. Fish is sold in this market .... eleven in the morning.
30. They jumped .... the top of the truck.
31. There is some bread lying .... the fridge.
32. There is some bread lying .... the table.
33. The bus was parked .... your house.
34. We enjoyed ourselves .... the vacation.
35. They open the office .... Saturday.
36. She will be in Chandigarh .... the last week of January.
37. She went to Jaipur .... taxi.
38. I opened the door .... your key.
39. There is no flight .... Guwahati .... Monday.
40. He cut this log of wood .... an axe.

Unit 54

PHRASAL VERBS

A phrasal verb in English is a combination of two or three words and has a single meaning. A phrasal verb of two words may consist of a verb + particle. The particle can be an adverb or a preposition.

(1) My car *broke down* on the main road.
(verb + adverb)

(2) He *got over* his failure in the examination.
(verb + preposition)

Intransitive verb + adverb

A phrasal verb (intransitive verb + adverb participle) can be intransitive, that is, it does not require an object after it but one can use an adverbial after it.

(3) My car *broke down* on the road.

Here *broke down* means *failed to work* or *stopped working.*

(4) I have given my refrigerator for repair as it *broke down* last week.

Catch on means to understand (used with people). For example,

(5) I couldn't *catch on* to her lecture.

EXERCISE 1 (ADVANCED)

Rewrite the following sentences. From the box, choose a suitable phrasal verb in the right grammatical form for the underlined words in each sentence. You may consult a dictionary.

break down	drag on	fall apart
break out	drop in	fall off
catch on	drop out	fall out
come down	doze off	fall through
stay up	turn up	get along
pass away	go on	set in
hold on	settle down	make off
stand out		

1. Autumn has already begun.
2. I do not have a cordial relationship with Vijaya.
3. They did not arrive at the conference venue.
4. They disagreed with each other on a petty matter.
5. He left the course after two months at the University.
6. The schedule ended without success after it was found that they were lying.
7. I remained awake last night because I had to finish my project.
8. Wait a minute, I'll see if Rakhee is around.
9. The General could be noticed among all the senior officers.
10. Her mother made a will before she died.
11. On seeing the police inspector, the thief escaped in a hurry.
12. John is sitting comfortably near the fireplace.
13. The meeting could not take place as many members objected to many items on the agenda.
14. We had to spend the night in a hotel because our bus stopped working on the way.
15. The statue may break into pieces as it has not been set properly.
16. She fell asleep during the concert.
17. He continued delivering his lecture even after the bell had rung.
18. The student enrolment has decreased this year.
19. This case has gone on slowly for ten years now.
20. The Second World War started suddenly in 1939.
21. I visited her without prior announcement and surprised her.
22. Our teacher has taught us grammar for six months but we have failed to understand it.

Transitive verb + adverb

This type of phrasal verb requires an object as an obligatory element.

(6) You can *switch on* the light.
(7) She *called up* John.

It is possible to use the object before the adverb participle in the above sentences.

(8) You can *switch* the light *on*.

If the object is a pronoun, it has to be used before the adverb.

(9) You can *fill* it *up*.
(10) She *called* him *up*.

EXERCISE 2 (ADVANCED)

Rewrite the following sentences choosing the correct phrasal verb to be used in place of the underlined words in each sentence making any other changes that may be necessary.

bring about	fill up	make up	step up
bring up	fix up	mess up	take down
carry out	give up	phase out	try out
cook up	hand over	pull down	wipe out
cross out	hush up	rule out	
draw up	knock down	see off	
fill in	look up	sort out	

1. The municipal corporation destroyed the old building to raise a new one.
2. Indian Oil Corporation has increased oil production in recent weeks.
3. He deleted the amount and wrote down a new figure on the cheque.
4. The war has completely destroyed the countryside.
5. I've arranged a meeting with the Managing Director.
6. They have prepared a plan to start a new construction company.
7. Mukesh invented a false story about his book.
8. I couldn't understand the last part of his speech.
9. Rakesh's mother educated and reared Rakesh with great love and care.
10. We gave our cabin baggage to the flight attendant on entering the plane.
11. I've saved a lakh for my son's college education.
12. She may complete this form for admission to the BCA course.
13. The Director has hidden the case regarding the kickbacks.
14. He can write whatever is dictated very fast.
15. We have tested this book in different countries.
16. You need to organise your luggage at the railway station.
17. All of us went to the railway station to say goodbye to our English teacher.
18. He completed his work to the satisfaction of his employer.
19. Please fill this glass with coke and ice cream.
20. You must find out the meaning of a word that you don't know in a dictionary.
21. Manish is planning to stop smoking.
22. His marriage caused a great change to his personality.
23. The national airline is going to stop using small aircraft.
24. The foreign minister has rejected any talks with the extremists.
25. He has spoiled the whole plan.

Intransitive verb + preposition

(11) I do not *approve of* his conduct.
(12) He will have to *account for* his silly behaviour.

Exercise 3 (Advanced)

Rewrite the following sentences. From the box, choose the correct phrasal verb to be used in place of the underlined words in each sentence. Make any other changes that may be necessary. You may use the dictionary.

bank on get over count on look into	fall for call on look after	break into laugh at dispose of

1. The Chief Minister himself examined the case as it concerned the security of the state.
2. She was attracted to the little child as soon as she entered the orphanage.
3. She can depend on her family for support.
4. She made fun of his stupidity.
5. We were relying on your support in the board election.
6. He has got rid of his old house.
7. She took care of our business when we were abroad.
8. It took years for her to recover from the death of her husband.
9. We visited the Vice-chancellor yesterday.
10. The thieves entered the house in the early hours on Monday.

Transitive verb + preposition

Phrasal verbs of this type are followed by two noun phrases. The first noun phrase is used after the transitive verb and is, therefore, the object of the verb. The second noun phrase is used after the preposition and is the object of the preposition.

(13) Germany *drew* many European countries into the war in 1939.
(14) Rakesh has *assured me of* financial assistance for starting the factory.

bank on	fall for	break into
get over	call on	take in
count on	look after	dispose of
look into		

4. He [illegible] made fun of his [illegible].